New Selec

C000126602

Also by Elizabeth Jennings available from Carcanet

In the Meantime

Tributes

Sonnets of Michelangelo *(translator)*

A Poet's Choice

New Collected Poems

Every Changing Shape: Mystical Experience
and the Making of Poems

ELIZABETH JENNINGS

New Selected Poems

Edited by Rebecca Watts

CARCANET

First published in Great Britain in 2019 by
Carcanet Press Ltd
Alliance House, 30 Cross Street
Manchester M2 7AQ
www.carcanet.co.uk

A CIP catalogue record for this book is available from the British Library.
ISBN 978 1 784108 65 6

The publisher acknowledges financial assistance from Arts Council England.

Typeset in England by XL Publishing Services, Exmouth
Printed and bound in England by SRP Ltd, Exeter

Contents

SONG FOR A BIRTH OR A DEATH (1961)

RECOVERIES (1964)

THE MIND HAS MOUNTAINS (1966)

THE ANIMALS' ARRIVAL (1969)

LUCIDITIES (1970)

RELATIONSHIPS (1972)

GROWING POINTS (1975)

CONSEQUENTLY I REJOICE (1977)

Times and Seasons (1992)

Familiar Spirits (1994)

In the Meantime (1996)

Praises (1998)

Timely Issues (2001)

Editor's Note

Forty years have passed since Carcanet first published Elizabeth Jennings's *Selected Poems*. In 1979 it was Jennings herself – in collaboration with her editor, Michael Schmidt – who made the selection, which comprised 103 poems chosen from among her first twelve collections of poetry (the books up to and including *Relationships*).

Honouring Jennings's choices, this volume preserves the contents of the 1979 *Selected Poems* in its entirety. I have added four poems from that period (including 'Old Woman', which Jennings elsewhere singled out as 'the best' of the portrait poems in *A Sense of the World*), and my additions are indicated by asterisks beside those poems' titles in the contents list.

The rest of this volume consists of my selections from the twelve collections and two pamphlets Jennings published after 1972 – beginning with *Growing Points*, Jennings's favourite of her collections, and ending with *Timely Issues*, which was brought to press shortly after her death in 2001. The text of the poems replicates that of the 2012 *Collected* edition, with the exception of a few minor adjustments to punctuation, made in the service of clarity and consistency.

As anyone acquainted with the *Collected Poems* or her biography will know, Jennings wrote prodigiously – compulsively, perhaps – and inevitably not all of her poems hit the same mark as the taut, inventive lyrics that launched her career as a poet and made her early books remarkable. From 1975 onwards, Michael Schmidt took charge of assembling Jennings's collections out of the masses of handwritten poems she submitted to him in spiral-bound notebooks. 'It was intensely exciting for me', Schmidt has noted, 'when a fine poem managed to burst free of the undergrowth […] to dazzle eye and ear.' It is my hope that, by showcasing a fraction of Jennings's colossal output, this *New Selected Poems* will allow readers already familiar with her work to be freshly dazzled, and enable a new generation of readers to encounter this surprising poet at her best.

Rebecca Watts
Cambridge, 2019

POEMS

1953

Delay

The radiance of the star that leans on me
Was shining years ago. The light that now
Glitters up there my eyes may never see,
And so the time lag teases me with how

Love that loves now may not reach me until
Its first desire is spent. The star's impulse
Must wait for eyes to claim it beautiful
And love arrived may find us somewhere else.

Winter Love

Let us have Winter loving that the heart
May be in peace and ready to partake
Of the slow pleasure Spring would wish to hurry
Or that in Summer harshly would awake,
And let us fall apart, O gladly weary,
The white skin shaken like a white snowflake.

Reminiscence

When I was happy alone, too young for love
Or to be loved in any but a way
Cloudless and gentle, I would find the day
Long as I wished its length or web to weave.

I did not know or could not know enough
To fret at thought or even try to whittle
A pattern from the shapeless stony stuff
That now confuses since I've grown too subtle.

I used the senses, did not seek to find
Something they could not touch, made numb with fear;
I felt the glittering landscape in the mind
And O was happy not to have it clear.

Fantasy

Tree without a leaf I stand
Bird unfeathered cannot fly
I a beggar weep and cry
Not for coins but for a hand

To beg with. All my leaves are down
Feathers flown and hand wrenched off
Bird and tree and beggar grown
Nothing on account of love.

Italian Light

It is not quite a house without the sun
And sun is what we notice, wonder at
As if stone left its hard and quarried state
To be reciprocal to light and let
The falling beams bound and rebound upon
Shutter and wall, each with assurance thrown.

So on descending from the snow we meet
Not warmth of south but houses which contrive
To be designed of sun. The builders have
Instructed hands to know where shadows fall
And made of buildings an obedient stone
Linked to the sun as waters to the moon.

Afternoon in Florence

This afternoon disturbs within the mind
No other afternoon, is out of time
Yet lies within a definite sun to end
In night that is in time. Yet hold it here
Our eyes, our minds, to make the city clear.

Light detains no prisoner here at all
In brick or stone but sends a freedom out,
Extends a shadow like a deeper thought,
Makes churches move, once still,
Rocking in light as music rocks the bell.

So eyes make room for light and minds make room
For image of the city tangible.
We look down on the city and a dream
Opens to wakefulness, and waking on
This peace perpetuates this afternoon.

Identity

When I decide I shall assemble you
Or, more precisely, when I decide which thoughts
Of mine about you fit most easily together,
Then I can learn what I have loved, what lets
Light through the mind. The residue
Of what you may be goes. I gather

Only as lovers or friends gather at all
For making friends means this –
Image and passion combined into a whole
Pattern within the loving mind, not her or his
Concurring there. You can project the full
Picture of lover or friend that is not either.

So then assemble me,
Your exact picture firm and credible,
Though as I think myself I may be free
And accurate enough.
That you love what is truthful to your will
Is all that ever can be answered for
And, what is more,
Is all we make each other when we love.

The Idler

An idler holds that rose as always rose,
Will not, before the bud discloses it
Within a later season, in his thought
Unwrap the flower and force the petals open
And wish in mind a different rose to happen.

So will not colour it with his own shadow
As we contrive, living beyond the present,
To move all things away from their own moment
And state another time for us. O who
Watches may yet make time refuse to grow.

So has his subtle power wiser than ours
And need elaborate no peace at all.
Watch how a landscape kindest is to idlers
Helping their shiftlessness grow to new powers,
Composing stillness round their careless will.

Bell-Ringer

The bells renew the town, discover it
And give it back itself again, the man
Pulling the rope collects the houses as
Thoughts gather in the mind·unscanned, he is
Crowding the town together from the night

And making bells the morning, in remote
Control of every life (for bells shout 'Wake'
And shake out dreams, though it is he who pulls
The sleep aside). But not into his thought
Do men continue as in lives of power;

For when each bell is pulled sufficiently
He never sees himself as any cause
Or need; the sounds had left his hands to sing
A meaning for each listening separately,
A separate meaning for the single choice.

Yet bells retire to silence, need him when
Time must be shown a lucid interval
And men look up as if the air were full
Of birds descending, bells exclaiming in
His hands but shouting wider than his will.

The Climbers

To the cold peak without their careful women
(Who watching children climbing into dreams
Go dispossessed at home). The mountain moves
Away at every climb and steps are hard
Frozen along the glacier. Every man
Tied to the rope constructs himself alone.

And not the summit reached nor any pole
Touched is the wished embrace, but still to move
And as the mountain climbs to see it whole
And each mind's landscape growing more complete
As sinews strain and all the muscles knot.

One at the peak is small. His disappointment
The coloured flag flown at the lonely top,
And all the valley's motive grown obscure.
He envies the large toilers halfway there
Who still possess the mountain by desire
And, not arriving, dream in no resentment.

Fishermen

This to be peace, they think beside the river
Being adapted well to expectation
And their wives' mutiny at no achievement,
And yet can sit watching the promises
Escape through weeds and make a trial of biting,
Can lose them, thankful that it is not yet
Time to draw in the line and drain the net.

Learning themselves in this uncertainty
Each hardly cares whether a fish is caught,
For here is privacy, each warns himself,
The fish, inquiries in the river, not
When drawn out promises at all
Being so solid on the bank and still.

Only the boys who live in certainty,
With expectation other than the stream,
Jeer at the patience and draw up their net
Of future frogs, the river vague to them
Until it's emptied. But the old men fill
Their eyes with water, leave the river full.

The Island

All travellers escape the mainland here.
The same geology torn from the stretch
Of hostile homelands is a head of calm,
And the same sea that pounds a foreign beach
Turns strangers here familiar, looses them
Kindly as pebbles shuffled up the shore.

Each brings an island in his heart to square
With what he finds, and all is something strange
But most expected. In this innocent air
Thoughts can assume a meaning, island strength
Is outward, inward, each man measures it,
Unrolls his happiness a shining length.

And this awareness grows upon itself,
Fastens on minds, is forward, backward, here.
The island focuses escape and free
Men on the shore are also islands, steer
Self to knowledge of self in the calm sea,
Seekers who are their own discovery.

A WAY OF LOOKING

1955

Poem in Winter

Today the children begin to hope for snow
And look in the sky for auguries of it.
It is not for such omens that we wait;
Our world may not be settled by the slow
Falling of flakes to lie across our thought.

And even if the snow comes down indeed
We still shall stand behind a pane of glass
Untouched by it, and watch the children press
Their image on the drifts the snow has laid
Upon a Winter they think they have made.

This is a wise illusion. Better to
Believe the near world is created by
A wish, a shaping hand, a certain eye,
Than hide in the mind's corner as we do
As though there were no world, no fall of snow.

Song at the Beginning of Autumn

Now watch this Autumn that arrives
In smells. All looks like Summer still;
Colours are quite unchanged, the air
On green and white serenely thrives.
Heavy the trees with growth and full
The fields. Flowers flourish everywhere.

Proust who collected time within
A child's cake would understand
The ambiguity of this –
Summer still raging while a thin
Column of smoke stirs from the land
Proving that Autumn gropes for us.

But every season is a kind
Of rich nostalgia. We give names –
Autumn and Summer, Winter, Spring –
As though to unfasten from the mind
Our moods and give them outward forms.
We want the certain, solid thing.

But I am carried back against
My will into a childhood where
Autumn is bonfires, marbles, smoke;
I lean against my window fenced
From evocations in the air.
When I said Autumn, Autumn broke.

Kings

You send an image hurrying out of doors
When you depose a king and seize his throne:
You exile symbols when you take by force.

And even if you say the power's your own,
That you are your own hero, your own king,
You will not wear the meaning of the crown.

The power a ruler has is how men bring
Their thoughts to bear upon him, how their minds
Construct the grandeur from the simple thing.

And kings prevented from their proper ends
Make a deep lack in men's imagining;
Heroes are nothing without worshipping,

Will not diminish into lovers, friends.

The Enemies

Last night they came across the river and
Entered the city. Women were awake
With lights and food. They entertained the band,
Not asking what the men had come to take
Or what strange tongue they spoke
Or why they came so suddenly through the land.

Now in the morning all the town is filled
With stories of the swift and dark invasion;
The women say that not one stranger told
A reason for his coming. The intrusion
Was not for devastation:
Peace is apparent still on hearth and field.

Yet all the city is a haunted place.
Man meeting man speaks cautiously. Old friends
Close up the candid looks upon their face.
There is no warmth in hands accepting hands;
Each ponders, 'Better hide myself in case
Those strangers have set up their homes in minds
I used to walk in. Better draw the blinds
Even if the strangers haunt in my own house.'

In This Time

If the myth's outworn, the legend broken,
   Useless even within the child's story
Since he sees well they now bring lights no longer
   Into our eyes: and if our past retreats
And blows away like dust along the desert,
   Not leading to our moment now at all,
Settling us in this place and saying 'Here
   In you I shall continue' – then what kind
Of lives have we? Can we make myths revive
   By breathing on them? Is there any taper
That will return the glitter to our eyes?

We have retreated inwards to our minds
   Too much, have made rooms there with all doors closed,
All windows shuttered. There we sit and mope
   The myth away, set by the lovely legends;
Hardly we hear the children shout outside.
   We only know a way to love ourselves,
Have lost the power that made us lose ourselves.
   O let the wind outside blow in again
And the dust come and all the children's voices.
   Let anything that is not us return.
Myths are the memories we have rejected
   And legends need the freedom of our minds.

Beyond Possession

Our images withdraw, the rose returns
To what it was before we looked at it.
We lift our look from where the water runs
And it's pure river once again, we write
No emblems on the trees. A way begins
Of living where we have no need to beat
The petals down to get the scent of rose
Or sign our features where the water goes.

All is itself. Each man himself entire,
Not even plucking out his thought, not even
Bringing a tutored wilfulness to bear
Upon the rose, the water. Each has given
Essence of water back to itself, essence of flower,
Till he is yoked to his own heart and driven
Inward to find a private kind of peace
And not a mind reflecting his own face.

Yet must go deeper still, must move to love
Where thought is free to let the water ride,
Is liberal to the rose giving it life
And setting even its own shadow aside;
Till flower and water blend with freedom of
Passion that does not close them in and hide
Their deepest natures; but the heart is strong
To beat with rose and river in one song.

Tribute

Sometimes the tall poem leans across the page
And the whole world seems near, a simple thing.
Then all the arts of mind and hand engage
To make the shadow tangible. O white
As silence is the page where words shall sing
And all the shadows be drawn into light.

And no one else is necessary then.
The poem is enough that joins me to
The world that seems too far to grasp at when
Images fail and words are gabbled speech:
At those times clarity appears in you,
Your mind holds meanings that my mind can reach.

Are you remote, then, when words play their part
With a fine arrogance within the poem?
Will the words keep all else outside my heart,
Even you, my test of life and gauge?
No, for you are that place where poems find room,
The tall abundant shadow on my page.

For a Child Born Dead

What ceremony can we fit
You into now? If you had come
Out of a warm and noisy room
To this, there'd be an opposite
For us to know you by. We could
Imagine you in lively mood

And then look at the other side,
The mood drawn out of you, the breath
Defeated by the power of death.
But we have never seen you stride
Ambitiously the world we know.
You could not come and yet you go.

But there is nothing now to mar
Your clear refusal of our world.
Not in our memories can we mould
You or distort your character.
Then all our consolation is
That grief can be as pure as this.

Communication

No use to speak, no good to tell you that
A love is worn away not by the one
Who leaves but by the one who stays and hopes,
Since you would rather have the hoping still
Than be yourself again. What can I say
Who know, better than you, the one who has
Moved on, away, not loving him at all?

And certainly to you I would relinquish
This knowledge held in other ways of feeling
Though dressed up in the properties of passion
Looked at by you. Something is deeply held
By me who never deeply searched at all
And we are not yet wise enough or subtle
To offer anyone a state of mind.

This the particular problem, and I search
A power over our general condition,
Where love is like a landscape we can change
And where desire may be transformed to friendship
If friendship gives the really wanted knowledge,
Where we can see the end and have the power
To take the journey there a different way,
And we can move our minds as we move houses:
Where love is more than lucky in the land.

Mirrors

Was it a mirror then across a room,
A crowded room of parties where the smoke
Rose to the ceiling with the talk? The glass
Stared back at me a half-familiar face
Yet something hoped for. When at last you came
It was as if the distant mirror spoke.

That loving ended as all self-love ends
And teaches us that only fairgrounds have
The right to show us halls of mirrors where
In every place we look we see our stare
Taunting our own identities. But love
Perceives without a mirror in the hands.

In the Night

Out of my window late at night I gape
And see the stars but do not watch them really,
And hear the trains but do not listen clearly;
Inside my mind I turn about to keep
Myself awake, yet am not there entirely.
Something of me is out in the dark landscape.

How much am I then what I think, how much what I feel?
How much the eye that seems to keep stars straight?
Do I control what I can contemplate
Or is it my vision that's amenable?
I turn in my mind, my mind is a room whose wall
I can see the top of but never completely scale.

All that I love is, like the night, outside,
Good to be gazed at, looking as if it could
With a simple gesture be brought inside my head
Or in my heart. But my thoughts about it divide
Me from my object. Now deep in my bed
I turn and the world turns on the other side.

Answers

I kept my answers small and kept them near;
Big questions bruised my mind but still I let
Small answers be a bulwark to my fear.

The huge abstractions I kept from the light;
Small things I handled and caressed and loved.
I let the stars assume the whole of night.

But the big answers clamoured to be moved
Into my life. Their great audacity
Shouted to be acknowledged and believed.

Even when all small answers build up to
Protection of my spirit, still I hear
Big answers striving for their overthrow

And all the great conclusions coming near.

A SENSE OF THE WORLD

1958

Old Woman

So much she caused she cannot now account for
As she stands watching day return, the cool
Walls of the house moving towards the sun.
She puts some flowers in a vase and thinks
   'There is not much I can arrange
In here and now, but flowers are suppliant

As children never were. And love is now
A flicker of memory, my body is
My own entirely. When I lie at night
I gather nothing now into my arms,
   No child or man, and where I live
Is what remains when men and children go.'

Yet she owns more than residue of lives
That she has marked and altered. See how she
Warns time from too much touching her possessions
By keeping flowers fed, by polishing
   Her fine old silver. Gratefully
She sees her own glance printed on grandchildren.

Drawing the curtains back and opening windows
Every morning now, she feels her years
Grow less and less. Time puts no burden on
Her now she does not need to measure it.
   It is acceptance she arranges
And her own life she places in the vase.

Old Man

His age drawn out behind him to be watched:
It is his shadow you may say. That dark
He paints upon the wall is his past self,
A mark he only leaves when he is still
   And he is still now always,
At ease and watching all his life assemble.

And he intends nothing but watching. What
His life has made of him his shadow shows –
Fine graces gone but dignity remaining,
While all he shuffled after is composed
   Into a curve of dark, of silences:
An old man tranquil in his silences.

And we move round him, are his own world turning,
Spinning it seems to him, leaving no shadow
To blaze our trail. We are our actions only:
He is himself, abundant and assured,
   All action thrown away,
And time is slowing where his shadow stands.

Taken by Surprise

Before, the anticipation, the walk merely
Under the oaks, (the afternoon crushed down
To his pressed footprints), noon surrendered, forgotten –
And the man moving, singular under the sun
With the hazel held in his hand lightly, lightly:
On the edge of his ear the lisp of the wind among
Untrembling leaves. Sun at the tips of the trees
Looked down, looked cold, and the man felt easy there.
His shadow seemed fitting as never before it was,
And the almost silence a space a man may enter
And be forgotten by all but his secret thoughts.
Then, something taking his fingers: 'Is it the wind?'
He thought and looked to see if the branches moved.
But nothing unusual stirred the trees, again
His fingers trembled, the hazel shook, he felt
Suddenly life in the twig as a woman feels
Abrupt and close the stir of the unborn child.
O and the afternoon was altered then;
Power from all quarters flung at him, silence broke
And deft but uneasy far in the back of his mind
A word like water shuddered, streams gushed and fountains
Rose as the hazel leapt from his mastered hand.

The Storm

Right in the middle of the storm it was.
So many winds were blowing none could tell
Which was the fiercest or if trees that bent
So smoothly to each impulse had been waiting
All of their growing-time for just that impulse
To prove how pliable they were. Beneath,
Beasts fled away through fern, and stiffest grasses,
Which bent like fluid things, made tidal motion.

These who had never met before but in
Calmest surroundings, found all shadows mingling;
No stance could be struck here, no peace attained,
And words blew round in broken syllables,
Half-meanings sounded out like trumpet blasts,
Decisive words were driven into hiding.
Yet some hilarity united them
And faces, carved and cleared by rain and lightning,
Stared out as if they never had been seen.

And children now, lost in the wood together,
Becoming the behaviour of the wind,
The way the light fell, learnt each other newly
And sudden gentleness was apprehended
Till the abating winds, the whole storm swerving
Into another quarter, left them standing
Unwild and watching in bewilderment
Their own delusive shadows slow and part.

Her Garden

Not at the full noon will she pick those flowers
For sudden shade indoors would make them wilt.
The petals would drop down on polished wood
Adding another element to decay
Which all her old rooms are infected with.

Only outside she can put off the course
Of her disease. She has the garden built
Within high walls so no one can intrude.
When people pass she only hears the way
Their footsteps sound, never their closer breath.

But in her borders she observes the powers
Of bud and branch, forgetting how she felt
When, blood within her veins like sap, she stood,
Her arms like branches bare above the day
And all the petals strewn along her path.

No matter now for she has bridged the pause
Between fruition and decay. She'll halt
A little in her garden while a mood
Of peace so fills her that she cannot say
Whether it is the flowers' life or her death.

Summer and Time

Now when the days descend
We do not let them lie
But ponder on the end,
How morning air drained dry
Of mist will but contend
Later with evening sky.

And so we mix up time.
Children, we say, ignore
Before and after, chime
Only the present hour.
But we are wrong, they climb
What time is aiming for

But beg no lastingness.
And it is we who try
In every hour to press
Befores and afters, sigh
All the great hour's success
And set the spoiling by.

Heavy the heat today,
Even the clocks seem slow.
But children make no play
With summers years ago.
It is we who betray
Who tease the sundial so.

At Noon

Lying upon my bed I see
Full noon at ease. Each way I look
A world established without me
Proclaims itself. I take a book
And flutter through the pages where
Sun leaps through shadows. And I stare

Straight through the words and find again
A world that has no need of me.
The poems stride against the strain
Of complex rhythms. Separately
I lie and struggle to become
More than a centre to this room.

I want the ease of noon outside,
Also the strength of words which move
Against their music. All the wide
And casual day I need to stuff
With my own meaning and the book
Of poems reflects me where I look.

Ghosts

Those houses haunt in which we leave
Something undone. It is not those
Great words or silences of love

That spread their echoes through a place
And fill the locked-up unbreathed gloom.
Ghosts do not haunt with any face

That we have known; they only come
With arrogance to thrust at us
Our own omissions in a room.

The words we would not speak they use,
The deeds we dared not act they flaunt,
Our nervous silences they bruise;

It is our helplessness they choose
And our refusals that they haunt.

Absence

I visited the place where we last met.
Nothing was changed, the gardens were well tended,
The fountains sprayed their usual steady jet;
There was no sign that anything had ended
And nothing to instruct me to forget.

The thoughtless birds that shook out of the trees,
Singing an ecstasy I could not share,
Played cunning in my thoughts. Surely in these
Pleasures there could not be a pain to bear
Or any discord shake the level breeze.

It was because the place was just the same
That made your absence seem a savage force,
For under all the gentleness there came
An earthquake tremor: fountain, birds and grass
Were shaken by my thinking of your name.

Disguises

Always we have believed
We can change overnight,
Put a different look on the face,
Old passions out of sight:
And find new days relieved
Of all that we regretted –
But something always stays
And will not be outwitted.

Say we put on dark glasses,
Wear different clothes and walk
With a new unpractised stride –
Always somebody passes
Undeceived by disguises
Or the different way we talk.
And we who could have defied
Anything if it was strange
Have nowhere we can hide
From those who refuse to change.

The Parting

Though there was nothing final then,
No word or look or sign,
I felt some ending in the air
As when a sensed design
Draws back from the completing touch
And dies along a line.

For through the words that seemed to show
That we were learning each
Trick of the other's thought and sense,
A shyness seemed to reach
As if such talk continuing
Would make the hour too rich.

Maybe this strangeness only was
The safe place all men make
To hide themselves from happiness;
I only know I lack
The strangeness our last meeting had
And try to force it back.

Resemblances

Always I look for some reminding feature,
Compel a likeness where there is not one,
As in a gallery I trace the stature
Of that one's boldness or of this one's grace.
Yet likenesses so searched for will yield none;
One feature, yes, but never the whole face.

So every face falls back into its parts
And once-known glances leave the candid look
Of total strangeness. Where the likeness starts
We fix attention, set aside the rest,
As those who scan for notes a thick-packed book,
Recalling only what has pleased them best.

And doing this, so often I have missed
Some recognition never known before,
Some knowledge which I never could have guessed.
And how if all the others whom I pass
Should like myself be always searching for
The special features only one face has?

Always the dear enchanted moment stays.
We cannot unlearn all whom we have loved;
Who can tear off like calendars the days
Or wipe out features fixed within the mind?
Only there should be some way to be moved
Beyond the likeness to the look behind.

A Death

'His face shone' she said,
'Three days I had him in my house,
Three days before they took him from his bed,
And never have I felt so close.'

'Always alive he was
A little drawn away from me.
Looks are opaque when living and his face
Seemed hiding something, carefully.'

'But those three days before
They took his body out, I used to go
And talk to him. That shining from him bore
No secrets. Living, he never looked or answered so.'

Sceptic, I listened, then
Noted what peace she seemed to have,
How tenderly she put flowers on his grave
But not as if he might return again
Or shine or seem quite close:
Rather to please us were the flowers she gave.

The Shot

The bullet shot me and I lay
So calm beneath the sun, the trees
Shook out their shadows in the breeze
Which carried half the sky away.

I did not know if I was dead,
A feeling close to sleep lay near
Yet through it I could see the clear
River and grass as if in bed

I lay and watched the morning come
Gentle behind the blowing stuff
Of curtains. But the pain was rough,
Not fitting to a sunlit room.

And I am dying, then, I thought.
I felt them lift me up and take
What seemed my body. Should I wake
And stop the darkness in my throat

And break the mist before my eyes?
I felt the bullet's leaps and swerves.
And none is loved as he deserves
And death is a disguise.

Song for a Departure

Could you indeed come lightly
Leaving no mark at all
Even of footsteps, briefly
Visit not change the air
Of this or the other room,
Have quick words with us yet be
Calm and unhurried here?

So that we should not need –
When you departed lightly
Even as swift as coming
Letting no shadow fall –
Changes, surrenders, fear,
Speeches grave to the last,
But feel no loss at all?

Lightest things in the mind
Go deep at last and can never
Be planned or weighed or lightly
Considered or set apart.
Then come like a great procession,
Touch hours with drums and flutes:
Fill all the rooms of our houses
And haunt them when you depart.

Choices

Inside the room I see the table laid,
Four chairs, a patch of light the lamp has made

And people there so deep in tenderness
They could not speak a word of happiness.

Outside I stand and see my shadow drawn
Lengthening the clipped grass of the cared-for lawn.

Above, their roof holds half the sky behind.
A dog barks bringing distances to mind.

Comfort, I think, or safety then, or both?
I warm the cold air with my steady breath.

They have designed a way to live and I,
Clothed in confusion, set their choices by:

Though sometimes one looks up and sees me there,
Alerts his shadow, pushes back his chair

And, opening windows wide, looks out at me
And close past words we stare. It seems that he

Urges my darkness, dares it to be freed
Into that room. We need each other's need.

Telling Stories

For M.

Telling you stories I forget that you
Already know the end
And I forget that I am building up
A world in which no piece must be put back
In the wrong place or time
Else you will make me go back to the start.

My scope for improvising will not ever
Deceive you into taking
A change of plan. You are so grounded in
Your absolutes, even the worlds we build
Of thin thoughts, lean ideas
You will not let us alter but expect

The thing repeated whole. Is this then what
We call your innocence –
This fine decision not to have things changed?
Is this your way of stopping clocks, of damming
The thrusting stream of time?
Has a repeated story so much power?

Such is the trust you have not in large things
But in the placing of
A verb, an adjective, a happy end.
The stories that we tell, we tell against
Ourselves then at the last
Since all the worlds we make we stand outside

Leaning on time and swayed about by it
While you stand firm within the fragile plot.

A Fear

Always to keep it in and never spare
Even a hint of pain, go guessing on,
Feigning a sacrifice, forging a tear
For someone else's grief, but still to bear
Inward the agony of self alone –

And all the masks I carry on my face,
The smile for you, the grave considered air
For you and for another some calm grace
When still within I carry an old fear
A child could never speak about, disgrace
That no confession could assuage or clear.

But once within a long and broken night
I woke and threw the shutters back for air
(The sudden moths were climbing to the light)
And from another window I saw stare
A face like mine still dream-bereft and white
And, like mine, shaken by a child's nightmare.

In a Foreign City

You cannot speak for no one knows
Your language. You must try to catch
By glances or by steadfast gaze
The attitude of those you watch.
No conversations can amaze:
Noises may find you but not speech.

Now you have circled silence, stare
With all the subtlety of sight.
Noise may trap ears but eye discerns
How someone on his elbow turns
And in the moon's long exile here
Touches another in the night.

The Roman Forum

Look at the Forum
Commanded now by Roman pines:
Walk down the ancient paths
Rubbed smooth by footprints in the past and now
Broken among the baths
And battered columns where the lizards go
In zig-zag movements like the lines
Of this decorum.

Not what the man
Who carved the column, reared the arch
Or shaped the buildings meant
Is what we marvel at. Perfection here
Is quite within our reach,
These ruins now are more than monument.
See how the houses disappear
Into a plan

Connived at by
Shadows of trees or light approved
By sun and not designed
By architects. Three columns eased away
From all support are moved
By how the shadows shake them from behind.
The pine trees droop their dark and sway
Swifter than eye

Can catch them all,
O and the heart is drawn to sense,
Eye and the mind are one.
The fragments here of former markets make
(Preserved by the intense
Glare of the Roman unremitting sun)
Such cities that the heart would break
And shadows fall

To see them pass.
Removed from Rome you, half-asleep,
Observe the shadows stray.
Above, the pines are playing with the light.
Dream now so dark and deep
That when you wake those columns, lucid, free,
Will burst like flowers into white
Springing from grass.

from *A Sense of the World* (1958)   45

A Conversation in the Gardens of the Villa Celimontana, Rome

For A.

Deeper the shadows underneath the pines
Than their own trunks and roots. Under the hard
Blue of the sky (a Roman blue, they say)
I watched the afternoon weave its designs
Lucid as crystal on this first June day.

The fountains softly displayed themselves. The grass,
Unpressed by footprints yet, looked cool and young;
Over the paths we saw our shadows pass
And in the air the glittering moments strung
Together like a brilliance under glass.

Suddenly to this fullness our words went
Talking of visionaries, of those men
Who make a stillness deeper than an act,
Who probe beyond a place where passion's spent
And apprehend by purest intellect.

You talked of this and in between your words
I sensed (still shadowed by my own warm flesh)
That you had known such apprehension and
Back in this garden where the pine trees stand
Held to that moment where all hungers hush.

Yes but the garden held a stillness too.
My mind could seize upon the pleasures there,
Yet in between the fountains and the grass,
The leaning pines, the overriding air,
I glimpsed a radiance where no shadows pass.

A Roman Window

After the griefs of night,
Over the doors of day,
Here by this windowsill
I watch the climbing light
As early footsteps steal
Enormous shadows away.

Tenderly from this height
I feel compassion come –
People pestered by hours,
The morning swung to sight
As all the city stirs
And trembles in my room.

So from a stance of calm,
A stepping out of sleep,
My shadow once again
Disperses in the warm
Day with its lives more deep
Than any pleasure or pain.

Fountain

Let it disturb no more at first
Than the hint of a pool predicted far in a forest,
Or a sea so far away that you have to open
Your window to hear it.
Think of it then as elemental, as being
Necessity,
Not for a cup to be taken to it and not
For lips to linger or eye to receive itself
Back in reflection, simply
As water the patient moon persuades and stirs.

And then step closer,
Imagine rivers you might indeed embark on,
Waterfalls where you could
Silence an afternoon by staring but never
See the same tumult twice.
Yes come out of the narrow street and enter
The full piazza. Come where the noise compels.
Statues are bowing down to the breaking air.

Observe it there – the fountain, too fast for shadows,
Too wild for the lights which illuminate it to hold,
Even a moment, an ounce of water back;
Stare at such prodigality and consider
It is the elegance here, it is the taming,
The keeping fast in a thousand flowering sprays,
That builds this energy up but lets the watchers
See in that stress an image of utter calm,
A stillness there. It is how we must have felt
Once at the edge of some perpetual stream,
Fearful of touching, bringing no thirst at all,
Panicked by no perception of ourselves
But drawing the water down to the deepest wonder.

San Paolo Fuori Le Mura, Rome

It is the stone makes stillness here. I think
There could not be so much of silence if
The columns were not set there rank on rank,
For silence needs a shape in which to sink
And stillness needs these shadows for its life.

My darkness throws so little space before
My body where it stands, and yet my mind
Needs the large echoing churches and the roar
Of streets outside its own calm place to find
Where the soft doves of peace withdraw, withdraw.

The alabaster windows here permit
Only suggestions of the sun to slide
Into the church and make a glow in it;
The battering daylight leaps at large outside
Though what slips here through jewels seems most fit.

And here one might in his discovered calm
Feel the great building draw away from him,
His head bent closely down upon his arm,
With all the sun subsiding to a dim
Past-dreamt-of peace, a kind of coming home.

For me the senses still have their full sway
Even where prayer comes quicker than an act.
I cannot quite forget the blazing day,
The alabaster windows or the way
The light refuses to be called abstract.

Letter from Assisi

Here you will find peace, they said,
Here where silence is so wide you hear it,
Where every church you enter is a kind
Continuing of thought,
Here there is ease.
Now on this road, looking up to the hill
Where the town looks severe and seems to say
There is no softness here, no sensual joy,
Close by the flowers that fling me back to England –
The bleeding poppy and the dusty vetch
And all blue flowers reflecting back the sky –
It is not peace I feel but some nostalgia,
So that a hand which draws a shutter back,
An eye which warms as it observes a child,
Hurt me with homesickness. Peace pales and withers.

The doves demur, an English voice divides
The distances. It is the afternoon,
But here siesta has no place because
All of the day is strung with silences.
Bells wound the air and I remember one
Who long ago confided how such ringing
Brought salt into their mouth, tears to their eyes.
I think I understand a mood like that:
Doves, bells, the silent hills, O all the trappings
We dress our plans of peace in fail me now.
I search some shadow wider than my own,
Some apprehension which requires no mood
Of local silence or a sense of prayer –
An open glance that looks from some high window
And illustrates a need I wish to share.

The Annunciation

Nothing will ease the pain to come
Though now she sits in ecstasy
And lets it have its way with her.
The angel's shadow in the room
Is lightly lifted as if he
Had never terrified her there.

The furniture again returns
To its old simple state. She can
Take comfort from the things she knows
Though in her heart new loving burns,
Something she never gave to man
Or god before, and this god grows

Most like a man. She wonders how
To pray at all, what thanks to give
And whom to give them to. 'Alone
To all men's eyes I now must go'
She thinks, 'And by myself must live
With a strange child that is my own.'

So from her ecstasy she moves
And turns to human things at last
(Announcing angels set aside).
It is a human child she loves
Though a god stirs beneath her breast
And great salvations grip her side.

Teresa of Avila

Spain. The wild dust, the whipped corn, earth easy for footsteps, shallow to starving seeds. High sky at night like walls. Silences surrounding Avila.

She, teased by questions, aching for reassurance. Calm in confession before incredulous priests. Then back – to the pure illumination, the profound personal prayer, the four waters.

Water from the well first, drawn up painfully. Clinking of pails. Dry lips at the well-head. Parched grass bending. And the dry heart too – waiting for prayer.

Then the water-wheel, turning smoothly. Somebody helping unseen. A keen hand put out, gently sliding the wheel. Then water and the aghast spirit refreshed and quenched.

Not this only. Other waters also, clear from a spring or a pool. Pouring from a fountain like child's play – but the child is elsewhere. And she, kneeling, cooling her spirit at the water, comes nearer, nearer.

Then the entire cleansing, utterly from nowhere. No wind ruffled it, no shadows slid across it. Her mind met it, her will approved. And all beyonds, backwaters, dry words of old prayers were lost in it. The water was only itself.

And she knelt there, waited for shadows to cross the light which the water made, waited for familiar childhood illuminations (the lamp by the bed, the candle in church, sun beckoned by horizons) – but this light was none of these, was only how the water looked, how the will turned and was still. Even the image of light itself withdrew, and the dry dust on the winds of Spain outside her halted. Moments spread not into hours but stood still. No dove brought the tokens of peace. She was the peace that her prayer had promised. And the silences suffered no shadows.

SONG FOR A BIRTH
OR A DEATH

1961

Song for a Birth or a Death

Last night I saw the savage world
And heard the blood beat up the stair;
The fox's bark, the owl's shrewd pounce,
The crying creatures – all were there,
And men in bed with love and fear.

The slit moon only emphasised
How blood must flow and teeth must grip.
What does the calm light understand,
The light which draws the tide and ship
And drags the owl upon its prey
And human creatures lip to lip?

Last night I watched how pleasure must
Leap from disaster with its will:
The fox's fear, the watch-dog's lust
Know that all matings mean a kill:
And human creatures kissed in trust
Feel the blood throb to death until

The seed is struck, the pleasure's done,
The birds are thronging in the air;
The moon gives way to widespread sun.
Yes but the pain still crouches where
The young fox and the child are trapped
And cries of love are cries of fear.

Family Affairs

No longer here the blaze that we'd engender
Out of pure wrath. We pick at quarrels now
As fussy women stitch at cotton, slow
Now to forget and too far to surrender.
The anger stops, apologies also.

And in this end-of-Summer, weighted calm
(Climate of mind, I mean), we are apart
Further than ever when we wished most harm.
Indifference lays a cold hand on the heart;
We need the violence to keep us warm.

Have we then learnt at last how to untie
The bond of birth, umbilical long cord,
So that we live quite unconnected by
The blood we share? What monstrous kind of sword
Can sever veins and still we do not die?

A Game of Chess

The quiet moves, the gently shaded room:
It is like childhood once again when I
Sat with a tray of toys and you would come
To take my temperature and make me lie
Under the clothes and sleep. Now peacefully

We sit above the intellectual game.
Pure mathematics seems to rule the board
Emotionless. And yet I feel the same
As when I sat and played without a word
Inventing kingdoms where great feelings stirred.

Is it that knight and king and small squat castle
Store up emotion, bring it under rule,
So that the problems now with which we wrestle
Seem simply of the mind? Do feelings cool
Beneath the order of an abstract school?

Never entirely, since the whole thing brings
Me back to childhood when I was distressed:
You seem the same who put away my things
At night, my toys and tools of childish lust.
My king is caught now in a world of trust.

My Grandmother

She kept an antique shop – or it kept her.
Among Apostle spoons and Bristol glass,
The faded silks, the heavy furniture,
She watched her own reflection in the brass
Salvers and silver bowls, as if to prove
Polish was all, there was no need of love.

And I remember how I once refused
To go out with her, since I was afraid.
It was perhaps a wish not to be used
Like antique objects. Though she never said
That she was hurt, I still could feel the guilt
Of that refusal, guessing how she felt.

Later, too frail to keep a shop, she put
All her best things in one long narrow room.
The place smelt old, of things too long kept shut,
The smell of absences where shadows come
That can't be polished. There was nothing then
To give her own reflection back again.

And when she died I felt no grief at all,
Only the guilt of what I once refused.
I walked into her room among the tall
Sideboards and cupboards – things she never used
But needed: and no finger-marks were there,
Only the new dust falling through the air.

In Praise of Creation

That one bird, one star,
The one flash of the tiger's eye
Purely assert what they are,
Without ceremony testify.

Testify to order, to rule –
How the birds mate at one time only,
How the sky is, for a certain time, full
Of birds, the moon sometimes cut thinly.

And the tiger trapped in the cage of his skin,
Watchful over creation, rests
For the blood to pound, the drums to begin,
Till the tigress' shadow casts

A darkness over him, a passion, a scent,
The world goes turning, turning, the season
Sieves earth to its one sure element
And the blood beats beyond reason.

Then quiet, and birds folding their wings,
The new moon waiting for years to be stared at here,
The season sinks to satisfied things –
Man with his mind ajar.

World I Have Not Made

I have sometimes thought how it would have been
if I had had to create the whole thing myself –
my life certainly but also something else;
I mean a world which I could inhabit freely,
ideas, objects, everything prepared;
not ideas simply as Plato knew them,
shadows of shadows, but more like furniture,
something to move around and live in,
something *I* had made. But still there would be
all that I hadn't made – animals, stars,
tides tugging against me, moon uncaring,
and the trying to love without reciprocity.
All this is here still. It is hard, hard,
even with free faith outlooking boundaries,
to come to terms with obvious suffering.
I live in a world I have not created
inward or outward. There is a sweetness
in willing surrender: I trail my ideas
behind great truths. My ideas are like shadows
and sometimes I consider how it would have been
to create a credo, objects, ideas
and then to live with them. I can understand
when tides most tug and the moon is remote
and the trapped wild beast is one with its shadow,
how even great faith leaves room for abysses
and the taut mind turns to its own requirings.

Harvest and Consecration

After the heaped piles and the cornsheaves waiting
To be collected, gathered into barns,
After all fruits have burst their skins, the sating
 Season cools and turns,
And then I think of something that you said
Of when you held the chalice and the bread.

I spoke of Mass and thought of it as close
To how a season feels which stirs and brings
Fire to the hearth, food to the hungry house
 And strange, uncovered things –
God in a garden then in sheaves of corn
And the white bread a way to be reborn.

I thought of priest as midwife and as mother
Feeling the pain, feeling the pleasure too,
 All opposites together,
Until you said no one could feel such passion
And still preserve the power of consecration.

And it is true. How cool the gold sheaves lie,
Rich without need to ask for any more
Richness. The seed, the simple thing must die
 If only to restore
Our faith in fruitful, hidden things. I see
The wine and bread protect our ecstasy.

A World of Light

Yes when the dark withdrew I suffered light
And saw the candles heave beneath their wax,
I watched the shadow of my old self dwindle
As softly on my recollection stole
A mood the senses could not touch or damage,
A sense of peace beyond the breathing word.

Day dawdled at my elbow. It was night
Within. I saw my hands, their soft dark backs
Keeping me from the noise outside. The candle
Seemed snuffed into a deep and silent pool:
It drew no shadow round my constant image
For in a dazzling dark my spirit stirred.

But still I questioned it. My inward sight
Still knew the senses and the senses' tracks,
I felt my flesh and clothes, a rubbing sandal,
And distant voices wishing to console.
My mind was keen to understand and rummage
To find assurance in the sounds I heard.

Then senses ceased and thoughts were driven quite
Away (no act of mine). I could relax
And feel a fire no earnest prayer can kindle;
Old parts of peace dissolved into a whole
And like a bright thing proud in its new plumage
My mind was keen as an attentive bird.

Yes, fire, light, air, birds, wax, the sun's own height
I draw from now, but every image breaks.
Only a child's simplicity can handle
Such moments when the hottest fire feels cool,
And every breath is like a sudden homage
To peace that penetrates and is not feared.

A Requiem

It is the ritual not the fact
That brings a held emotion to
Its breaking-point. This man I knew
Only a little, by his death
Shows me a love I thought I lacked
And all the stirrings underneath.

It is the calm, the solemn thing,
Not the distracted mourner's cry
Or the cold place where dead things lie,
That teaches me I cannot claim
To stand aside. These tears which sting –
Are they from sorrow or from shame?

The Resurrection

I was the one who waited in the garden
Doubting the morning and the early light.
I watched the mist lift off its own soft burden,
Permitting not believing my own sight.

If there were sudden noises I dismissed
Them as a trick of sound, a sleight of hand.
Not by a natural joy could I be blessed
Or trust a thing I could not understand.

Maybe I was a shadow thrown by one
Who, weeping, came to lift away the stone,
Or was I but the path on which the sun,
Too heavy for itself, was loosed and thrown?

I heard the voices and the recognition
And love like kisses heard behind thin walls.
Were they my tears which fell, a real contrition
Or simply April with its waterfalls?

It was by negatives I learnt my place.
The garden went on growing and I sensed
A sudden breeze that blew across my face.
Despair returned but now it danced, it danced.

Mantegna's Agony in the Garden

The agony is formal; three
Bodies are stretched in pure repose,
One's halo leans against a tree,
Over a book his fingers close:
One's arms are folded carefully.

The third man lies with sandalled feet
Thrust in the path. They almost touch
Three playful rabbits. Down the street
Judas and his procession march
Making the distance seem discreet.

Even the praying figure has
A cared-for attitude. This art
Puts down the city and the mass
Of mountains like a counterpart
Of pain disguised as gentleness.

And yet such careful placing here
Of mountain, men and agony,
Being so solid, makes more clear
The pain. Pain is particular.
The foreground shows a barren tree:
Is it a vulture crouching there,
No symbol but a prophecy?

Visit to an Artist

For David Jones

Window upon the wall, a balcony
With a light chair, the air and water so
Mingled you could not say which was the sun
And which the adamant yet tranquil spray.
But nothing was confused and nothing slow:
Each way you looked always the sea, the sea.

And every shyness that we brought with us
Was drawn into the pictures on the walls.
It was so good to sit quite still and lose
Necessity of discourse, words to choose
And wonder which were honest and which false.

Then I remembered words that you had said
Of art as gesture and as sacrament,
A mountain under the calm form of paint
Much like the Presence under wine and bread –
Art with its largesse and its own restraint.

Lazarus

It was the amazing white, it was the way he simply
Refused to answer our questions, it was the cold pale glance
Of death upon him, the smell of death that truly
Declared his rising to us. It was no chance
Happening, as a man may fill a silence
Between two heartbeats, seem to be dead and then
Astonish us with the closeness of his presence;
This man was dead, I say it again and again.
All of our sweating bodies moved towards him
And our minds moved too, hungry for finished faith.
He would not enter our world at once with words
That we might be tempted to twist or argue with:
Cold like a white root pressed in the bowels of earth
He looked, but also vulnerable – like birth.

The Diamond Cutter

Not what the light will do but how he shapes it
And what particular colours it will bear,

And something of the climber's concentration
Seeing the white peak, setting the right foot there.

Not how the sun was plausible at morning
Nor how it was distributed at noon,

And not how much the single stone could show
But rather how much brilliance it would shun;

Simply a paring down, a cleaving to
One object, as the stargazer who sees

One single comet polished by its fall
Rather than countless, untouched galaxies.

Stargazers and Others

One, staring out stars,
Lost himself in looking and almost
Forgot glass, eye, air, space;
Simply, he thought, the world is improved
By my staring, how the still glass leaps
When the sky thuds in like tides.

Another, making love, once
Stared so far over his pleasure
That woman, world, the spiral
Of taut bodies, the clinging hands, broke apart
And he saw, as the stargazer sees,
Landscapes made to be looked at,
Fruit to fall, not be plucked.

In you also something
Of such vision occurs.
How else would I have learnt
The tapered stars, the pause
On the nervous spiral? Names I need
Stronger than love, desire,
Passion, pleasure. O discover
Some star and christen it, but let me be
The space that your eye moves over.

To a Friend with a Religious Vocation

For C.

Thinking of your vocation, I am filled
With thoughts of my own lack of one. I see
Within myself no wish to breed or build
Or take the three vows ringed by poverty.
    And yet I have a sense,
Vague and inchoate, with no symmetry,
Of purpose. Is it merely a pretence,

A kind of scaffolding which I erect
Half out of fear, half out of laziness?
The fitful poems come but can't protect
The empty areas of loneliness.
    You know what you must do,
So that mere breathing is a way to bless.
Dark nights, perhaps, but no grey days for you.

Your vows enfold you. I must make my own;
Now this, now that, each one empirical.
My poems move from feelings not yet known,
And when the poem is written I can feel
    A flash, a moment's peace.
The curtain will be drawn across your grille.
My silences are always enemies.

Yet with the same convictions that you have
(It is but your vocation that I lack),
I must, like you, believe in perfect love.
It is the dark, the dark that draws me back
    Into a chaos where
Vocations, visions fail, the will grows slack
And I am stunned by silence everywhere.

Greek Statues

These I have never touched but only looked at.
If you could say that stillness meant surrender
These are surrendered.
Yet their large audacious gestures signify surely
Remonstrance, reprisal? What have they left to lose
But the crumbling away by rain or time? Defiance
For them is a dignity, a declaration.

Odd how one wants to touch not simply stare,
To run one's fingers over the flanks and arms,
Not to possess, rather to be possessed.
Bronze is bright to the eye but under the hands
Is cool and calming. Gods into silent metal:

To stone also, not to the palpable flesh.
Incarnations are elsewhere and more human,
Something concerning us; but these are other.
It is as if something infinite, remote
Permitted intrusion. It is as if these blind eyes
Exposed a landscape precious with grapes and olives:
And our probing hands move not to grasp but praise.

The Pride of Life: A Roman Setting

Old men discourse upon wise topics here:
Children and women pass the shadows by,
   Only the young are desperate. Their clear
And unambiguous gazes strike
   Against each brushing hand or eye,
     Their faces like

   O something far away, maybe a cave
Where looks and actions always moved to hunt,
   Where every gesture knew how to behave
And there was never space between
   The easy having and the want.
     I think the keen

   Primitive stares that pierce this decorous street
Look to some far-back mood and time to claim
   A life beyond the urbane and effete
Where youth from coolest childhood came,
   And look to look was like the hunter's throw –
     Perpetually new and long ago.

Men Fishing in the Arno

I do not know what they are catching,
I only know that they stand there, leaning
A little like lovers, eager but not demanding,
Waiting and hoping for a catch, money,
A meal tomorrow but today, still there, steady.

And the river also moves as calmly
From the waterfall slipping to a place
A mind could match its thought with.
And above, the cypresses with cool gestures
Command the city, give it formality.

It is like this every day but more especially
On Sundays; every few yards you see a fisherman,
Each independent, none
Working with others and yet accepting
Others. From this one might, I think,

Build a whole way of living – men in their mazes
Of secret desires yet keeping a sense
Of order outwardly, hoping
Not too flamboyantly, satisfied with little
Yet not surprised should the river suddenly
Yield a hundredfold, every hunger appeased.

Two Deaths

It was only a film,
Perhaps I shall say later
Forgetting the story, left only
With bright images – the blazing dawn
Over the European ravaged plain,
And a white unsaddled horse, the only calm
Living creature. Will only such pictures remain?

Or shall I see
The shot boy running, running
Clutching the white sheet on the washing line,
Looking at his own blood like a child
Who never saw blood before and feels defiled,
A boy dying without dignity
Yet brave still, trying to stop himself from falling
And screaming – his white girl waiting just out of calling?

I am ashamed
Not to have seen anyone dead,
Anyone I know I mean;
Odd that yesterday also
I saw a broken cat stretched on a path,
Not quite finished. Its gentle head
Showed one eye staring, mutely beseeching
Death, it seemed. All day
I have thought of death, of violence and death,
Of the blazing Polish light, of the cat's eye:
I am ashamed I have never seen anyone die.

About These Things

About these things I always shall be dumb.
Some wear their silences as more than dress,
As more than skin-deep. I bear mine like some

Scar that is hidden out of shamefulness.
I speak from depths I do not understand
Yet cannot find the words for this distress.

So much of power is put into my hand
When words come easily. I sense the way
People are charmed and pause; I seem to mend

Some hurt. Some healing seems to make them stay.
And yet within the power that I use
My wordless fears remain. Perhaps I say

In lucid verse the terrors that confuse
In conversation. Maybe I am dumb
Because if fears were spoken I would lose

The lovely languages I do not choose
More than the darknesses from which they come.

The Instrument

Only in our imaginations
The act is done, for you have spoken
Vows that can never now be broken.
I keep them too – with reservations;
Yet acts not done can still be taken
Away, like all completed passions.

But what can not be taken is
Satiety. Cool space lies near
Our bodies – a parenthesis
Between a pleasure and a fear.
Our loving is composed of this
Touching of strings to make sounds clear.

A touching, then a glancing off.
It is your vows that stretch between
Us like an instrument of love
Where only echoes intervene.
Yet these exchanges are enough
Since strings touched only are most keen.

Remembering Fireworks

Always as if for the first time we watch
The fireworks as if no one had ever
Done this before, made shapes, signs,
Cut diamonds on air, sent up stars
Nameless, imperious. And in the falling
Of fire, the spent rocket, there is a kind
Of nostalgia as normally only attaches
To things long known and lost. Such an absence,
Such emptiness of sky the fireworks leave
After their festival. We, fumbling
For words of love, remember the rockets,
The spinning wheels, the sudden diamonds,
And say with delight 'Yes, like that, like that.'
Oh and the air is full of falling
Stars surrendered. We search for a sign.

RECOVERIES

1964

Sequence in Hospital

I Pain

At my wits' end
And all resources gone, I lie here,
All of my body tense to the touch of fear,
And my mind,

Muffled now as if the nerves
Refused any longer to let thoughts form,
Is no longer a safe retreat, a tidy home,
No longer serves

My body's demands or shields
With fine words, as it once would daily,
My storehouse of dread. Now, slowly,
My heart, hand, whole body yield

To fear. Bed, ward, window begin
To lose their solidity. Faces no longer
Look kind or needed; yet I still fight the stronger
Terror – oblivion – the needle thrusts in.

II The Ward

One with the photographs of grandchildren,
Another with discussion of disease,

Another with the memory of her garden,
Another with her marriage – all of these

Keep death at bay by building round their illness
A past they never honoured at the time.

The sun streams through the window, the earth heaves
Gently for this new season. Blossoms climb

Out in the healthy world where no one thinks
Of pain. Nor would these patients wish them to;

The great preservers here are little things –
The dream last night, a photograph, a view.

III   After an Operation

What to say first? I learnt I was afraid,
Not frightened in the way that I had been
When wide awake and well. I simply mean
Fear became absolute and I became
Subject to it; it beckoned, I obeyed.

Fear which before had been particular,
Attached to this or that scene, word, event,
Here became general. Past, future meant
Nothing. Only the present moment bore
This huge, vague fear, this wish for nothing more.

Yet life still stirred and nerves themselves became
Like shoots which hurt while growing, sensitive
To find not death but further ways to live.
And now I'm convalescent, fear can claim
No general power. Yet I am not the same.

IV Patients in a Public Ward

Like children now, bed close to bed,
With flowers set up where toys would be
In real childhoods, secretly
We cherish each our own disease,
And when we talk we talk to please
Ourselves that still we are not dead.

All is kept safe – the healthy world
Held at a distance, on a rope,
Where human things like hate and hope
Persist. The world we know is full
Of things we need, unbeautiful
And yet desired – a glass to hold

And sip, a cube of ice, a pill
To help us sleep. Yet in this warm
And sealed-off nest, the least alarm
Speaks clear of death. Our fears grow wide;
There are no places left to hide
And no more peace in lying still.

V The Visitors

They visit me and I attempt to keep
A social smile upon my face. Even here
Some ceremony is required, no deep
Relationship, simply a way to clear
    Emotion to one side; the fear
I felt last night is buried in drugged sleep.

They come and all their kindness makes me want
To cry (they say the sick weep easily).
When they have gone I shall be limp and faint,
My heart will thump and stumble crazily;
    Yet through my illness I can see
One wish stand clear no pain, no fear can taint.

Your absence has been stronger than all pain
And I am glad to find that when most weak
Always my mind returned to you again.
Through all the noisy nights when, harsh awake,
    I longed for day and light to break –
In that sick desert, you were life, were rain.

VI Hospital

Observe the hours which seem to stand
Between these beds and pause until
A shriek breaks through the time to show
That humankind is suffering still.

Observe the tall and shrivelled flowers,
So brave a moment to the glance.
The fevered eyes stare through the hours
And petals fall with soft footprints.

A world where silence has no hold
Except a tentative small grip.
Limp hands upon the blankets fold,
Minds from their bodies slowly slip.

Though death is never talked of here,
It is more palpable and felt –
Touching the cheek or in a tear –
By being present by default.

The muffled cries, the curtains drawn,
The flowers pale before they fall –
The world itself is here brought down
To what is suffering and small.

The huge philosophies depart,
Large words slink off, like faith, like love.
The thumping of the human heart
Is reassurance here enough.

Only one dreamer going back
To how he felt when he was well,
Weeps under pillows at his lack
But cannot tell, but cannot tell.

VII   For a Woman with a Fatal Illness

The verdict has been given and you lie quietly
Beyond hope, hate, revenge, even self-pity.

You accept gratefully the gifts – flowers, fruit –
Clumsily offered now that your visitors too

Know you must certainly die in a matter of months.
They are dumb now, reduced only to gestures,

Helpless before your news, perhaps hating
You because you are the cause of their unease.

I, too, watching from my temporary corner,
Feel impotent and wish for something violent –

Whether as sympathy only, I am not sure –
But something at least to break the terrible tension.

Death has no right to come so quietly.

VIII   Patients

Violence does not terrify.
Storms here would be a relief,
Lightning be a companion to grief.
It is the helplessness, the way they lie

Beyond hope, fear, love,
That makes me afraid. I would like to shout,
Crash my voice into the silence, flout
The passive suffering here. They move

Only in pain, their bodies no longer seem
Dependent on blood, muscle, bone.
It is as if air alone
Kept them alive, or else a mere whim

On the part of instrument, surgeon, nurse.
I too am one of them, but well enough
To long for some simple sign of life,
Or to imagine myself getting worse.

Man in a Park

One lost in thought of what his life might mean
Sat in a park and watched the children play,
Did nothing, spoke to no one, but all day
Composed his life around the happy scene.

And when the sun went down and keepers came
To lock the gates, and all the voices were
Swept to a distance where no sounds could stir,
This man continued playing his odd game.

Thus, without protest, he went to the gate,
Heard the key turn and shut his eyes until
He felt that he had made the whole place still,
Being content simply to watch and wait.

So one can live, like patterns under glass,
And, like those patterns, not committing harm.
This man continued faithful to his calm,
Watching the children playing on the grass.

But what if someone else should also sit
Beside him on the bench and play the same
Watching and counting, self-preserving game,
Building a world with him no part of it?

If he is truthful to his vision he
Will let the dark intruder push him from
His place, and in the softly gathering gloom
Add one more note to his philosophy.

Father to Son

I do not understand this child
Though we have lived together now
In the same house for years. I know
Nothing of him, so try to build
Up a relationship from how
He was when small. Yet have I killed

The seed I spent or sown it where
The land is his and none of mine?
We speak like strangers, there's no sign
Of understanding in the air.
This child is built to my design
Yet what he loves I cannot share.

Silence surrounds us. I would have
Him prodigal, returning to
His father's house, the home he knew,
Rather than see him make and move
His world. I would forgive him too,
Shaping from sorrow a new love.

Father and son, we both must live
On the same globe and the same land.
He speaks: I cannot understand
Myself, why anger grows from grief.
We each put out an empty hand,
Longing for something to forgive.

Warning to Parents

Save them from terror; do not let them see
The ghost behind the stairs, the hidden crime.
They will, no doubt, grow out of this in time
And be impervious as you and me.

Be sure there is a night-light close at hand;
The plot of that old film may well come back,
The ceiling, with its long, uneven crack,
May hint at things no child can understand.

You do all this and are surprised one day
When you discover how the child can gloat
On Belsen and on tortures – things remote
To him. You find it hard to watch him play

With thoughts like these, and find it harder still
To think back to the time when you also
Caught from the cruel past a childish glow
And felt along your veins the wish to kill.

Fears are more personal than we had guessed –
We only need ourselves; time does the rest.

Admonition

Watch carefully. These offer
Surprising statements, are not
Open to your proper doubt,
Will watch you while you suffer.

Sign nothing but let the vague
Slogans stand without your name.
Your indifference they claim
Though the issues seem so big.

Signing a paper puts off
Your responsibilities.
Trust rather your own distress
As in, say, matters of love.

Always behind you, judges
Will have something trite to say.
Let them know you want delay;
No star's smooth at its edges.

from *Recoveries* (1964)   85

The Young Ones

They slip on to the bus, hair piled up high.
New styles each month, it seems to me. I look,
Not wanting to be seen, casting my eye
Above the unread pages of a book.

They are fifteen or so. When I was thus,
I huddled in school coats, my satchel hung
Lopsided on my shoulder. Without fuss
These enter adolescence; being young

Seems good to them, a state we cannot reach,
No talk of 'awkward ages' now. I see
How childish gazes staring out of each
Unfinished face prove me incredibly

Old-fashioned. Yet at least I have the chance
To size up several stages – young yet old,
Doing the twist, mocking an 'old-time' dance:
So many ways to be unsure or bold.

Bewilderment

Not to enter the haunted house,
Not to let the talkers go too deep,
Not to travel without maps, and not
To analyse one's restless sleep –
Is this then cowardice and shamed refusal?

To say we need to go away,
To shout we cannot listen any more,
To travel only well-known streets;
When strangers come, to lock the door –
What judgment will be passed on this?

To be open always to experience,
To welcome change and newness, eager talk,
To give oneself away in conversation,
Never to use the map but always walk
Calm into darkness. Is this wisdom?

I do not know the answers, yet I ask
Myself these questions over and over again.
Is this willingness to ask itself perhaps
A way to live? Is the house haunted then
Only with dust and dark and silences?

THE MIND HAS MOUNTAINS

1966

In a Mental Hospital Sitting-Room

Utrillo on the wall. A nun is climbing
Steps in Montmartre. We patients sit below.
It does not seem a time for lucid rhyming;
Too much disturbs. It does not seem a time
When anything could fertilise or grow.

It is as if a scream were opened wide,
A mouth demanding everyone to listen.
Too many people cry, too many hide
And stare into themselves. I am afraid.
There are no lifebelts here on which to fasten.

The nun is climbing up those steps. The room
Shifts till the dust flies in between our eyes.
The only hope is visitors will come
And talk of other things than our disease …
So much is stagnant and yet nothing dies.

Madness

Then this is being mad; there is no more
Imagining, Ophelias of the mind.
This girl who shouts and slobbers on the floor,
Sending us frightened to the corner, is
To all the world we know now deaf and blind
And we are merely loathsome enemies.

It is the lack of reason makes us fear,
The feeling that ourselves might be like this.
We are afraid to help her or draw near
As if she were infectious and could give
Some taint, some touch of her own fantasies,
Destroying all the things for which we live.

And, worse than this, we hate the madness too
And hate the mad one. Measured off a space
There is a world where things run calm and true –
But not for us. We have to be with her
Because our minds are also out of place
And we have carried more than we can bear.

from *The Mind Has Mountains* (1966)   89

The Interrogator

He is always right.
However you prevaricate or question his motives,
Whatever you say to excuse yourself
He is always right.

He always has an answer.
It may be a question that hurts to hear,
It may be a sentence that makes you flinch.
He always has an answer.

He always knows best.
He can tell you why you disliked your father,
He can make your purest motive seem aggressive.
He always knows best.

He can always find words.
While you fumble to feel for your own position
Or stammer out words that are not quite accurate,
He can always find words.

And if you accuse him
He is glad you have lost your temper with him.
He can find the motive, give you a reason
If you accuse him.

And if you covered his mouth with your hand,
Pinned him down to his smooth desk chair,
You would be doing just what he wishes.
His silence would prove that he was right.

Attempted Suicides

We have come back.
Do not be surprised if we blink our eyes
If we stare oddly
If we hide in corners.
It is we, not you, who should show surprise.

For everything looks strange.
Roofs are made of paper
Hands are muslin
Babies look eatable.
There has been too much change.

And where do we come from?
Where did the pills take us,
The gas,
The water left pouring?
Limbo? Hell? Mere forgetfulness?

It was a lost moment,
There were no dreams,
There was simply the beyond-endurance
And then the coming-to
To you and you and you and you.

Do not ask us,
As if we were Lazarus,
What it was like.
We never got far enough.
Now we touch ourselves and feel strange.
We have a whole world to arrange.

Night Sister

How is it possible not to grow hard,
To build a shell around yourself when you
Have to watch so much pain, and hear it too?
Many you see are puzzled, wounded; few
Are cheerful long. How can you not be scarred?

To view a birth or death seems natural,
But these locked doors, these sudden shouts and tears
Graze all the peaceful skies. A world of fears
Like the ghost-haunting of the owl appears.
And yet you love that stillness and that call.

You have a memory for everyone;
None is anonymous and so you cure
What few with such compassion could endure.
I never met a calling quite so pure.
My fears are silenced by the things you've done.

We have grown cynical and often miss
The perfect thing. Embarrassment also
Convinces us we cannot dare to show
Our sickness. But you listen and we know
That you can meet us in our own distress.

Words from Traherne

'You cannot love too much, only in the wrong way.'

It seemed like love; there were so many ways
Of feeling, thinking, each quite separate.
Tempers would rise up in a sudden blaze,
Or someone coming twitch and shake the heart.

Simply, there was no calm. Fear often came
And intervened between the quick expression
Of honest movements or a kind of game.
I ran away at any chance of passion.

But not for long. Few can avoid emotion
So powerful, although it terrifies.
I trembled, yet I wanted that commotion
Learnt through the hand, the lips, the ears, the eyes.

Fear always stopped my every wish to give.
I opted out, broke hearts, but most of all
I broke my own. I would not let it live
Lest it should make me lose control and fall.

Now generosity, integrity,
Compassion too, are what make me exist,
Yet still I cannot come to terms or try,
Or even know, the knot I must untwist.

Samuel Palmer and Chagall

You would have understood each other well
And proved to us how periods of art
Are less important than the personal
Worlds that each painter makes from mind and heart.

The greatest – Blake, Picasso – move about
In many worlds. You only have one small
Yet perfect place. In it, there is no doubt,
And no deception can exist at all.

Great qualities make such art possible,
A sense of truth, integrity, a view
Of man that fits into a world that's whole,
Those moons, those marriages, that dark, that blue.

I feel a quiet in it all although
The subject and the scenes are always strange.
I think it is that order pushes through
Your images, and so you can arrange

And make the wildest, darkest dream serene;
Landscapes are like still-lives which somehow move,
The moon and sun shine out of the same scene –
Fantastic worlds but all are built from love.

On a Friend's Relapse and Return to a Mental Clinic

I had a feeling that you might come back,
And dreaded it.
You are a friend, your absence is a lack;
I mean now that

We do not meet outside the hospital:
You are too ill
And I, though free by day, cannot yet call
Myself quite well.

Because of all of this, it was a shock
To find that you
Were really bad, depressed, withdrawn from me
More than I knew.

You ask for me and sometimes I'm allowed
To go and sit
And gently talk to you – no noise too loud;
I'm glad of it.

You take my hand, say odd things, sometimes weep,
And I return
With rational talk until you fall asleep.
So much to learn

Here; there's no end either at second-hand
Or else within
Oneself, or both. I want to understand
But just begin

When something startling, wounding comes again.
Oh heal my friend.
There should be peace for gentle ones, not pain.
Bring her an end

Of suffering, or let us all protest
And realise
It is the good who often know joy least.
I fight against the size

And weight of such a realisation, would
Prefer no answers trite
As this; but feeling that I've understood,
I can accept, not fight.

Night Garden of the Asylum

An owl's call scrapes the stillness.
Curtains are barriers and behind them
The beds settle into neat rows.
Soon they'll be ruffled.

The garden knows nothing of illness.
Only it knows of the slow gleam
Of stars, the moon's distilling; it knows
Why the beds and lawns are levelled.

The all is broken from its fullness.
A human cry cuts across a dream.
A wild hand squeezes an open rose.
We are in witchcraft, bedevilled.

A Depression

She left the room undusted, did not care
To hang a picture, even lay a book
On the small table. All her pain was there –
In absences. The furious window shook
With violent storms she had no power to share.

Her face was lined, her bones stood thinly out.
She spoke, it's true, but not as if it mattered;
She helped with washing-up and things like that.
Her face looked anguished when the china clattered.
Mostly she merely stared at us and sat.

And then one day quite suddenly she came
Back to the world where flowers and pictures grow
(We sensed that world though we were much the same
As her). She seemed to have the power to know
And care and treat the whole thing as a game.

But will it last? Those prints upon her walls,
Those stacks of books – will they soon disappear?
I do not know how a depression falls
Or why so many of us live in fear.
The cure, as much as the disease, appals.

Grove House, Iffley

For Vivien

Your house is full of objects that I prize –
A marble hand, paperweights that uncurl,
Unfolding endlessly to red or blue.
Each way I look, some loved thing meets my eyes,
And you have used the light outside also;
The Autumn gilds collections old and new.

And yet there is no sense of *objets d'art*,
Of rarities just valued for their worth.
The handsome objects here invite one's touch,
As well as sight. Without the human heart,
They'd have no value, would not say so much.
Something of death belongs to them – and birth.

Nor are they an escape for anyone.
Simply you've fashioned somewhere that can give
Not titillation, pleasure, but a sense
Of order and of being loved; you've done
What few can do who bear the scars and prints
Of wounds from which they've learnt a way to live.

Chinese Art

You said you did not care for Chinese art
Because you could not tell what dynasty
A scroll or bowl came from. 'There is no heart'
You said, 'Where time's avoided consciously.'

I saw your point because I loved you then.
The willows and the horses and the birds
Seemed cold to me; each skilfully laid-on, thin
Phrase spoke like nothing but unpassionate words.

I understand now what those artists meant;
They did not care for style at all, or fashion.
It was eternity they tried to paint,
And timelessness, they thought, must lack all passion.

Odd that just when my feeling need for you
Has gone all wrong, I should discover this.
Yes, but I lack the sense of what is true
Within these wise old artists' skilfulness.

It would be easy now to close again
My heart against such hurt. Those willows show,
In one quick stroke, a lover feeling pain,
And birds escape fast as the brush-strokes go.

Love Poem

There is a shyness that we have
Only with those whom we most love.
Something it has to do also
With how we cannot bring to mind
A face whose every line we know.
O love is kind, O love is kind.

That there should still remain the first
Sweetness, also the later thirst –
This is why pain must play some part
In all true feelings that we find
And every shaking of the heart.
O love is kind, O love is kind.

And it is right that we should want
Discretion, secrecy, no hint
Of what we share. Love which cries out,
And wants the world to understand,
Is love that holds itself in doubt.
For love is quiet, and love is kind.

One Flesh

Lying apart now, each in a separate bed,
He with a book, keeping the light on late,
She like a girl dreaming of childhood,
All men elsewhere – it is as if they wait
Some new event: the book he holds unread,
Her eyes fixed on the shadows overhead.

Tossed up like flotsam from a former passion,
How cool they lie. They hardly ever touch,
Or if they do it is like a confession
Of having little feeling – or too much.
Chastity faces them, a destination
For which their whole lives were a preparation.

Strangely apart, yet strangely close together,
Silence between them like a thread to hold
And not wind in. And time itself's a feather
Touching them gently. Do they know they're old,
These two who are my father and my mother
Whose fire, from which I came, has now grown cold?

THE ANIMALS' ARRIVAL

1969

The Animals' Arrival

So they came
Grubbing, rooting, barking, sniffing,
Feeling for cold stars, for stone, for some hiding place,
Loosed at last from heredity, able to eat
From any tree or from ground, merely mildly themselves,
And every movement was quick, was purposeful, was proposed.
The galaxies gazed on, drawing in their distances.
The beasts breathed out warm on the air.

No one had come to make anything of this,
To move it, name it, shape it a symbol;
The huge creatures were their own depth, the hills
Lived lofty there, wanting no climber.
Murmur of birds came, rumble of underground beasts
And the otter swam deftly over the broad river.

There was silence too.
Plants grew in it, it wove itself, it spread, it enveloped
The evening as day-calls died and the universe hushed, hushed.
A last bird flew, a first beast swam
And prey on prey
Released each other
(Nobody hunted at all):
They slept for the waiting day.

Never to See

Never to see another evening now
With that quick openness, that sense of peace
That, any moment, childhood could allow.

Never to see the Spring and smell the trees
Alone, with nothing asking to come in
And shake the mind, and break the hour of ease –

All this has gone since childhood began
To go and took with it those tears, that rage.
We can forget them now that we are men.

But what will comfort us in our old age?
The feeling little, or the thinking back
To when our hearts were their own privilege?

It will be nothing quiet, but the wreck
Of all we did not do will fill our lack
As the clocks hurry and we turn a page.

Bonnard

Colour of rooms. Pastel shades. Crowds. Torsos at ease in
brilliant baths. And always, everywhere the light.

This is a way of creating the world again, of seeing differences,
of piling shadow on shadow, of showing up distances, of bringing
close, bringing close.

A way of furnishing too, of making yourself feel at home – and
others. Pink, flame, coral, yellow, magenta – extreme colours
for ordinary situations. This is a way to make a new world.

Then watch it. Let the colours dry, let the carpets collect a
little dust. Let the walls peel gently, and people come, innocent,
nude, eager for bed or bath.

They look newmade too, these bodies, newborn and innocent.
Their flesh-tints fit the bright walls and floors and they take
a bath as if entering the first stream, the first fountain.

A Letter to Peter Levi

Reading your poems I am aware
Of translucencies, of birds hovering
Over estuaries, of glass being spun for huge domes.
I remember a walk when you showed me
A tablet to Burton who took his own life.
You seem close to fragility yet have
A steel-like strength. You help junkies,
You understand their language,
You show them the stars and soothe them.
You take near-suicides and talk to them.
You are on the strong side of life, yet also the brittle;
I think of blown glass sometimes but reject the simile.
Yet about your demeanour there is something frail,
The strength is within, won from simple things
Like swimming and walking.
Your pale face is like an icon, yet
Any moment, any hour, you break to exuberance,
And then it is our world which is fragile:
You toss it like a juggler.

Any Poet's Epitaph

It does this, I suppose – protects
From the rough message, coarseness, grief,
From the sigh we would rather not hear too much,
And from our own brief gentleness too.

Poetry – builder, engraver, destroyer,
We invoke you because like us
You are the user of words; the beasts
But build, mate, destroy, and at last
Lie down to old age or simply sleep.

Coins, counters, Towers of Babel,
Mad words spoken in sickness too –
All are considered, refined, transformed,
On a crumpled page or a wakeful mind,
And stored and given back – and true.

LUCIDITIES

1970

Considerations

Some say they find it in the mind,
A reason why they should go on.
Others declare that they can find
The same in travel, art well done.

Still others seek in sex or love
A reciprocity, relief.
And few, far fewer daily, give
Themselves to God, a holy life.

But poetry must change and make
The world seem new in each design.
It asks much labour, much heartbreak,
Yet it can conquer in a line.

First Evening, by Rimbaud

She was half-undressed;
A few indiscreet trees
Threw out their shadows and displayed
Their leaves, cunningly and close.

She sat, half-naked in my chair,
She clasped her hands,
And her small feet shook
Where the floor bends.

I watched, on her lips
And also on her breast
A stray light flutter
And come to rest.

First, it was her ankles I kissed;
She laughed gently, and then
Like a bird she sang
Again and again.

Her feet withdrew and,
In an odd contradiction
She said 'Stop, do.'
Love knows such affliction.

I kissed her eyes.
My lips trembled, so weak.
Then she opened her lips again and said,
'There are words I must speak.'

This was too much, too much.
I kissed her breast and, at once,
She was tender to my touch.
She did not withdraw or wince.

Her clothes had fallen aside,
But the great trees threw out their leaves.
I am still a stranger to love,
Yet this was one of my loves.

The Rooks, by Rimbaud

When the meadow is cold, Lord, and when
The Angelus is no longer heard,
I beg you to let it come,
This delightful kind of bird –
The rook – and here make its home.
One, many, sweep down from the skies.

Such an odd army – you birds.
You have very strange voices.
Cold winds attack your nests,
Yet come, I implore, as if words
Were your medium. Where the river rests,
Dry and yellow, by Crosses

And ditches, come forward, come
In your thousands, over dear France
Where many are still asleep.
This is truly your home.
Wheel over so that a chance
Traveller may see the deep

Meaning within you all.
Be those who show men their duty,
And also reveal the world's beauty.
You, all of you
(And I know this is true)
Are the dark attendants of a funeral.

You, saints of the sky,
Of the oak tree, of the lost mast,
Forget about those of the Spring,
Bring back hope to the lost
Places, to those who feel nothing
But that defeat is life's cost.

RELATIONSHIPS

1972

Friendship

Such love I cannot analyse;
It does not rest in lips or eyes,
Neither in kisses nor caress.
Partly, I know, it's gentleness

And understanding in one word
Or in brief letters. It's preserved
By trust and by respect and awe.
These are the words I'm feeling for.

Two people, yes, two lasting friends.
The giving comes, the taking ends.
There is no measure for such things.
For this all Nature slows and sings.

A Sonnet

Run home all clichés, let the deep words come
However much they hurt and shock and bruise.
There is a suffering we can presume,
There is an anger, also, we can use;
There are no categories for what I know
Hunted by every touch on memory.
A postcard can produce a heartbreak blow
And sentiment comes seething when I see
A photograph, a Christmas card or some
Association with this loss, this death.
I must live through all this and, with no home
But what he was, keep holding on to breath.
Once the stars shone within a sky I knew.
Now only darkness is my sky, my view.

Let Things Alone

You have to learn it all over again,
The words, the sounds, almost the whole language
Because this is a time when words must be strict and new
Not concerning you,
Or only indirectly,
Concerning a pain
Learnt as most people some time or other learn it
With shock, then dark.

The flowers will refer to themselves always
But should not be loaded too much
With meaning from happier days.
They must remain themselves,
Dear to the touch.
The stars also
Must go on shining without what I now know.
And the sunset must simply glow.

Hurt

They do not mean to hurt, I think,
People who wound and still go on
As if they had not seen the brink

Of tears they forced or even known
The wounding thing. I'm thinking of
An incident. I brought to one,

My host, a present, small enough
But pretty and picked out with care.
I put it in her hands with love,

Saying it came from Russia; there
Lay my mistake. The politics
Each of us had, we did not share.

But I am not immune to lack
Like this in others; she just thrust
The present over, gave it back

Saying, 'I do not want it.' Must
We hurt each other in such ways?
This kind of thing is worse than Lust

And other Deadly Sins because
It's lack of charity. For this,
Christ sweated blood, and on the Cross

When every nail was in its place,
Though God himself, he called as man
At the rejection. On his face

Among the sweat, there must have been
Within the greater pain, the one
A hurt child shows, the look we can

Detect and feel, swift but not gone,
Only moved deeper where the heart
Stores up all things that have been done

And, though forgiven, don't depart.

GROWING POINTS

1975

Beech

They will not go. These leaves insist on staying.
Coinage like theirs looked frail six weeks ago.
What hintings at, excitement of delaying,
Almost as if some richer fruits could grow

If leaves hung on against each swipe of storm,
If branches bent but still did not give way.
Today is brushed with sun. The leaves are warm.
I picked one from the pavement and it lay

With borrowed shining on my Winter hand.
Persistence of this nature sends the pulse
Beating more rapidly. When will it end,

That pride of leaves? When will the branches be
Utterly bare, and seem like something else,
Now half-forgotten, no part of a tree?

Grapes

Those grapes, ready for picking, are the sign
Of harvest and of Sacrament. Do not
Touch them; wait for the ones who tread the wine,
See Southern air surround that bunch, that knot

Of juice held in. In Winter vines appear
Pitiful as a scarecrow. No one would
Guess from their crippled and reluctant air
That such refreshment, such fermenting could

Come from what seem dry bones left after death.
But, look now, how those pregnant bunches hang,
Swinging upon a pendulum of breath,

Intense small globes of purple till the hour
Of expert clipping comes. There is a pang
In seeing so much fullness change its power.

Thunder and a Boy

For T.

That great bubble of silence, almost tangible quiet was shattered.
                                    There was no prelude, the huge chords
Broke and sounded timpani over the town, and then lightning, first
                                            darting, then strong bars
    Taking hold of the sky, taking hold of us as we sank into primitive
                                                    people,
Wondering at and frightened of the elements, forgetting so swiftly how
                                    naming had once seemed
    To give them into our hands. Not any longer. We were powerless
                                        now completely.

But today we have risen with the rain and, though it is torrential, we
                                    believe at moments that we
Still have power over that. We are wrong. Those birds escaping through
                                        showers show us
    They are more imperial than we are. We shift, talk, doze, look at
                                                papers,
Though one child is remembering how last night he stood with defiance

    And joy at his window and shouted, 'Do it again, God, do it again!'
Can we say he was less wise than us? We cannot. He acknowledged Zeus,
    Thor, God the Father, and was prepared to cheer or dispute with any
                                                of them.
This afternoon he watches the sky, praying the night will show God's
                                        strength again
    And he, without fear, feel those drums beating and bursting through
                                his defended, invisible mind.

I Feel

I feel I could be turned to ice
If this goes on, if this goes on.
I feel I could be buried twice
And still the death not yet be done.

I feel I could be turned to fire
If there can be no end to this.
I know within me such desire
No kiss could satisfy, no kiss.

I feel I could be turned to stone,
A solid block not carved at all,
Because I feel so much alone.
I could be gravestone or a wall.

But better to be turned to earth
Where other things at least can grow.
I could be then a part of birth,
Passive, not knowing how to know.

After a Time

For a friend dead two years

I have not stood at this grave nor have I
Been where men come at last to silence when
Death sends them to instinctive ceremony,
Whether in torturing sun or fitting rain,
Whether they stare or cry.

What do I say who never put a wreath
Down for a father or this friend? Someone
Will make the speech for me. O this dear death,
Two years of missing all have been undone,
Yet I am growing with

Spontaneous strengths, blessings I did not claim –
Laughter, a child, knowledge of justice and
Faith like a cross which oddly bears my name,
Falls round my neck. In early hours I stand
Reflecting how I came

To this. What takes me through the corridors
Of grief? Was it the touch of love, that leading thread
Which drew me to glad grief from wrong remorse,
Wiped off the dust and let me see the dead
With new care now, new laws?

Rembrandt's Late Self-Portraits

You are confronted with yourself. Each year
The pouches fill, the skin is uglier.
You give it all unflinchingly. You stare
Into yourself, beyond. Your brush's care
Runs with self-knowledge. Here

Is a humility at one with craft.
There is no arrogance. Pride is apart
From this self-scrutiny. You make light drift
The way you want. Your face is bruised and hurt
But there is still love left.

Love of the art and others. To the last
Experiment went on. You stared beyond
Your age, the times. You also plucked the past
And tempered it. Self-portraits understand,
And old age can divest,

With truthful changes, us of fear of death.
Look, a new anguish. There, the bloated nose,
The sadness and the joy. To paint's to breathe,
And all the darknesses are dared. You chose
What each must reckon with.

Losing and Finding

You had been searching quietly through the house
That late afternoon, Easter Saturday,
And a good day to be out of doors. But no,
I was reading in a north room. You knocked
On my door once only, despite the dark green notice,
'Do not disturb'. I went at once and found you,

Paler than usual, not smiling. You just said
'I've lost them'. That went a long way back
To running, screaming through a shop and knocking
Against giants. 'I haven't had lunch', you said.
I hadn't much food and the shop was closed for Easter
But I found two apples and washed them both for you.

Then we went across the road, not hand in hand.
I was wary of that. You might have hated it
And anyway you were talking and I told you
About the river not far off, how some people
Swam there on a day like this. And how good the grass
Smelt as we walked to the recreation ground.

You were lively now as I spun you lying flat,
Talking fast when I pushed you on the swing,
Bold on the chute but obedient when, to your question
About walking up without hands, I said 'Don't. You'll fall.'
I kept thinking of your being lost, not crying,
But the sense of loss ran through me all the time

You were chatting away. I wanted to keep you safe,
Not know fear, be curious, love people
As you showed me when you jumped on my lap one evening,
Hugged me and kissed me hard. I could not keep you
Like that, contained in your joy, showing your need
As I wished *I* could. There was something elegiac

Simply because this whole thing was direct,
Chance, too, that you had found me when your parents
So strangely disappeared. There was enchantment
In the emptiness of that playground so you could
Be free for two hours only, noted by me, not you.
An Easter Saturday almost gone astray

Because you were lost and only six years old.
And it was you who rescued me, you know.
Among the swings, the meadow and the river,
You took me out of time, rubbed off on me
What it feels like to care without restriction,
To trust and never think of a betrayal.

An Abandoned Palace

A palace where the courtiers have vanished fleetly because
The work was too hard, and where they squabbled continually about
                                                    their rights
    And the Queen's debt to them – this has foundered as if the close sea
                                                            had
Rolled over and entered the doors. People ran out screaming.
    Two stayed – an old woman bound to rheumatic fingers and the now
                                                            hard
Embroidery she insisted on finishing. The other was the undeposed but
                                                    rejected and
    Uncomplaining Queen, who did not mind that the crown was covered
With mildew, the jewels were sold. She was subdued into a soft, slow,
    Ever-expanding melancholy, though her eyes smiled,
Bidding farewell to the servants gone, asking only that
    The steward should remain, add up the valuables and
Sell them. Then, in the high bedroom, she sat thinking

    Of utter simplicities, the heir who had gone to travel the world and
                                                            had not
Written. In her notebook she wrote two words only, two words
    Of disfigured defiance meaning almost total loss. The words were
'Find me.' Quickly she took a moulting carrier pigeon to trust this
                                                    message to
    And, with careful hands, glided the bird out of the tarnished windows
                                                    and then
Sat, waiting, occasionally visiting the trembling old woman, admiring
    The progress of the stitching, herself hiding tears, still, somehow,
                                                    hoping for
Rescue, reprieve, an escape from a palace now a prison where hope itself
    Taunted her continually with its expert disappointments,
Its refusal to gaze back at her long, caught in its own desperate incapacity.

Observing

That tree across the way
Has been a magnet to me all this year.
What happens to it is what interests me.
   I've watched a blackbird stay
Glued for a moment, unglue, disappear.
Violence came in April to that tree,
   Made its whole being sway

   Till I was sure it could
Not stand, would snap and in torn fragments lie,
Leaving another entrance for the sky.
   But that frail-seeming wood,
A conifer with intricate small leaves,
Stands under stars now while a new moon conceives
   Itself before the eye.

CONSEQUENTLY I REJOICE

1977

Restlessness

Houses whose dirt and hurt we've kicked off gladly
Soon become perfect in the memory.
Guitars in next-door rooms, a record badly
Scratched or put on too high
Dwindle away and somewhere else we see
And miss that view, that always sunset sky.

This moving which had seemed not only vital
But also something to look forward to
Is retrogressive and we cannot settle
In elsewhere very long.
Houses are only moods which we move through.
Too late we learn that most first moves were wrong.

Almost Drowning

First there was coming,
A coming-to, a sense of giddy
Limbs, another's or wings gleaming
Across the light. I was the body.
Was air or earth unsteady?

Second were voices,
Syllables, vowels were turning, running
Together. I was having races
With these, to overtake their meaning.
Then one word about drowning.

Third was the sea,
The tear of it about me still,
The time in it never to be
Within my compass or my will,
A birth or death writ small.

Better Than a Protest

Tear off the rags of all my loves; you'll find
The scarecrow which you see
Was fashioned long ago in your own mind,
It was not made by me.
Blow tempests on my treasures. When you pick
Sharp pebbles up, treat them with care. You see
You're dazzled by my jewels, the pile is thick.

Remember that the berries and the flowers
You took indoors to die
Have their own strange recuperative powers.
I took them up. They lie
Sprouting already in my hands. I'm quick
To push them in the ground until a tree
Drops healing herbs for you, new buds for me.

Let There Be

Let there be dark for us to contemplate.
Light draws the senses. O that seize of stars
Or even ember-comfort in a grate –

These blind us. Christ, teach us the *Book of Hours*
Which says 'Be silent' as we turn the page
And let the vigil come. Light overpowers.

Give us the night, the lonely privilege
Of offering our praise, a plea within
Enormous spaces lasting to the edge

Of almost dawn, and let the birds begin
To chip at sounds, set fire to tree and hedge.

Hatching

His night has come to an end and now he must break
The little sky which shielded him. He taps
Once and nothing happens. He tries again
And makes a mark like lightning. He must thunder,
Storm and shake and break a universe
Too small and safe. His daring beak does this.

And now he is out in a world of smells and spaces.
He shivers. Any air is wind to him.
He huddles under wings but does not know
He is already shaping feathers for
A lunge into the sky. His solo flight
Will bring the sun upon his back. He'll bear it,
Carry it, learn the real winds, by instinct
Return for food and, larger than his mother,
Avid for air, harry her with his hunger.

The Sleep of Birds

We cannot hear the birds sleeping
Under the trees, under the flowers, under the eyes of our watching
And the rustling over of sheets of our unsleeping
Or our final whispers of loving.
How enviable this solemn silence of theirs
Like the quiet of monks tired with their singing hours
And dreaming about the next.
Birds are remote as stars by being silent
And will flash out like stars at their punctual dawn
As the stars are snuffed by the sun.

Does this quiet sleep of birds hide dreams, hide nightmares?
Does the lash of wind and the failing wing and the falling
Out of the air enter their sleep? Let us listen,
Open the window and listen
For a cry of a nightmare to underline the night.
There is no cry, there is only
The one feathered life who's not awake and does not sing
But hoots and holds his own, his own now being
A lordly and humorous comment upon the darkness,
A quiet joke at the changing demands of the moon.

Ways of Dying

Shall we go bird-like down out of the air
Falling, falling, vertigo feeling only
Shaking our minds as they slowly blur, blur
And flesh is soon to be finally dust and lonely?

Or shall we scream and roar and make a scene
Like a nursery one, yelling 'It is unjust.
So much I meant to do, so much not seen'
And long for hunger and anger again and lust?

Or shall we lie quietly hoping to keep
The stranger's grip from stopping our hearts' slow beating
Or disappear in the corridors of sleep
But for what darkness there or for what meeting?

Christ Seen by Flemish Painters

Never the loaves and fishes multiplied,
Never the senses loosed, never the full
Attentive crowd, bloat faces set beside
A landscape opulent with sun and whole
Terraces hung with wide

Sweet fruit. Austerity, the grey face drawn,
The body almost spirit on the wood,
The wood like ash. Perhaps two lookers torn
By watching night through with no sleep or food.
Yes, here God is alone.

And man has seen the solitude of spaces,
The no-star air, the soil which hurts the feet,
The puckered pain on hands, the worried faces,
Triumphant anguish just before defeat,
The cool air of hard graces.

MOMENTS OF GRACE

1979

Into the Hour

I have come into the hour of a white healing.
Grief's surgery is over and I wear
The scar of my remorse and of my feeling.

I have come into a sudden sunlit hour
When ghosts are scared to corners. I have come
Into the time when grief begins to flower

Into a new love. It had filled my room
Long before I recognised it. Now
I speak its name. Grief finds its good way home.

The apple blossom's handsome on the bough
And Paradise spreads round. I touch its grass.
I want to celebrate but don't know how.

I need not speak though everyone I pass
Stares at me kindly. I would put my hand
Into their hands. Now I have lost my loss

In some way I may later understand.
I hear the singing of the Summer grass
And love, I find, has no considered end,

Nor is it subject to the wilderness
Which follows death. I am not traitor to
A person or a memory. I trace

Behind that love another which is running
Around, ahead. I need not ask its meaning.

Flies

All through the Winter these tunnel
Torpid air, desert of central heating,
Doubling men's thirst. These live God
Knows where, and they are his creatures.
Buzz, buzz, they insist,
Flies fallen from Summer,
Jig-zagging from cupboards, appearing
At the first left toffee,
And the smoking Christmas cake.

They carry dirt, we know,
They are ugly. They cannot help it.
Aesop would have a message. Creatures are good
For our metaphorical questions
And our necessary teaching.
I will try to admire this toss of a cigarette burning,
Bringing destruction and pain
But being so dogged with it.
'Let the flies come still,' I say
And let no one else complain.

Cat in Winter

Evader mostly, a glancing cold, a watcher
Of snow from a warm distance, a clever seeker
Of the heated corner, the generous lap, the fingers
Handing tit-bits or filling a shallow saucer –

So the cat in Winter and his movements.
He slinks into hiding places like a dandy
Recovering from a party or preparing
For another appearance in the evening. This one,
Striped, ginger and handsome,

Is a teller of weather, has a machine in his head
Which is a barometer to him. He is inventive,
Enterprising always, always lucky.
We sink into February and its inertia.
The cat's ears are cocked for a Spring of happy hunting.

Forgiveness

Anger, pity, always, most, forgive.
It is the word which we surrender by,
It is the language where we have to live,

For all torn tempers, sulks and brawls at last
Lie down in huge relief as if the world
Paused on its axis. Sorrow does sound best

When whispered near a window which can hold
The full moon or its quarter. Love, I say,
In spite of many hours when I was cold

And obdurate I never meant to stay
Like that or, if I meant to, I can't keep
The anger up. Our storms must draw away,

Their durance is not long. Almost asleep,
I listen now to winds' parley with trees
And feel a kind of comforting so deep

I want to share it. This unpaid-for peace
Possesses me. How much I wish to give
Some back to you, but living's made of these

Moments when every anger comes to grief
And we are rich in right apologies.

Channel Port Night

Boats signal nothing but night.
This English Channel port town is only eyes
Of green and red and yellow. Tide is in.
Waves keep calm. Only the gulls' cries
Insist on being heeded. Now we begin
  A dream-voyage under the light

Of little ships and houses. Being near
The rugged clangour of the anchored ships
Tells us swimmers that our dreams will be
Constant with voyages. Love, I touch your lips
And taste their salt. Do the same now to me
  Before the night's *détour*.

Thought and Feeling

I have grown wary of the ways of love
And when I find a moment crammed with thought
I cherish that sweet coolness and I move

As only spirits can, as dryads caught
In a Greek grove, then loosed among the trees.
Worship does not mean passion, I was taught.

But I have been brought down upon my knees;
Was it by prayer or by the ancient church
In which I found both art and artifice?

I do not know but I know I must touch
And that it is by flesh the spirit lives.
The strides of mind are prisoned in the reach

Of sense so intricate that it receives
All impressions, sieves them as a beach
Takes worn-down, random stones and offers them

To any wanderer there on his way home.

Death

They did not speak of death
But went round and round the subject deviously.
    They were out of breath
With keeping it at bay. When would they see
    That they were burdened with

    Dying like other men?
Immediate mourners know the whole of grief
    When they've seen the dying in pain
And the gradual move toward the end of life.
    O death comes again and again

And starts with the crying child and the doctor's knife.

Night Power

Am I alone now as the wind comes up
Sweeping huge stretches of the darkened sky,
Threading the stars, enfolding others' sleep?

I am yet am not. In this room that's high
Above a formal garden far away
From crowds and noise, I am the lonely cry

Of owls who tell the hours. I rule the day
As my mind reaches for before-dawn peace
And there is reason in the words I say

Or write. How warm it is. The bluff winds sing
The rise in temperature. I think the end
Of Winter's come, but now is neither Spring

Nor any other season while I stand,
As if the globe were trembling in my hand
And I could still the world's fraught whispering.

Christmas Suite in Five Movements

1 The Fear

So simple, very few
Can be so bare, be open to the wide
Dark, the starless night, the day's persistent
Wearing away of time. See, men cast off
Their finery and lay it on the floor,

Here, of a stable. What do they wait for?
Answers to learned questions? No, they have
Been steeped in books and wear the dust of them.

Philosophy breaks all its definitions,
Logic is lost, and here
The Word is silent. This God fears the night,
A child so terrified he asks for us.
God is the cry we thought came from our own
Perpetual sense of loss.
Can God be frightened to be so alone?
Does that child dream the Cross?

2 The Child

Blood on a berry,
    Night of frost.
Some make merry.
    Some are lost.

Footsteps crack
    On a pool of ice.
Hope is back.
    This baby lies

Wrapped in rags,
    Is fed by a girl.
O if God begs,
    Then we all hold

Him in our power.
    We catch our breath.
This is the hour
    For the terrible truth,

Terrible, yes,
    But sweet also.
God needs us.
    Now, through snow,

Tomorrow through heat
    We carry him
And hear his heart
    And bring him home.

3 A Litany

Mary of solace, take our hope,
Girl untouched, take our hands,
Lady of Heaven, come to our homes,
You bring Heaven down.

Mary of mercy, learn our laws,
Lady of care, take impulse to
Your heart, give us grace,
More than enough
And a relish for
The renewal of love.

Queen of formal gardens, reach our forests,
Girl of the fountains, come into our desert.
Mary of broken hearts, help us to keep
Promises. Lady of wakefulness, take our sleep.
You hold God in your arms and he may weep.

4 The Despair

All night you fought the dream and when you woke
Lay exhausted, blinded by the sun.
How could you face the day which had begun?
As we do, Christ, but worse for you. You broke
Into our history. History drives you on.

Love before this was dust, but it was dust
You took upon yourself. Your empty hands
Have scars upon them. You have made amends
For all wrong acts, for love brought down to lust.
God, the world is crying and man stands

Upon the brink of worse than tragedy.
That was noble. Now there's something more
Than careful scenes and acts. Some men make war
On you and we feel helpless, are not free
To struggle for you. God, we've seen you poor

And cold. Are stars dispensing light that you
Should find the universe turned … can it be
Away from you? No, no, we cannot see
Far or fully. Christ, just born, you go
Back to the blighted, on to the thriving Tree.

5 The Victory

Down to that littleness, down to all that
Crying and hunger, all that tiny flesh
And flickering spirit – down the great stars fall,
Here the huge kings bow.
Here the farmer sees his fragile lambs,
Here the wise man throws his books away.

This manger is the universe's cradle,
This singing mother has the words of truth.
Here the ox and ass and sparrow stop,
Here the hopeless man breaks into trust.
God, you have made a victory for the lost.
Give us this daily Bread, this little Host.

A DREAM OF SPRING

1980

Winter Argument

It was a rife and perfect Winter cold,
The scarecrow oaks stood out against the sky.
The sun gave half an hour of melting gold
While rooks were grounded. Who lives in this island
For long will never for its mildness cry.
You pull your own place up, hand by rough hand.

You take the weather and tear pages up,
Those chapters full of faulty forecasts and
The massive edges of a rotten crop.
Better expect too little than too much.
What was a feverish is now a spent land,
And yet it yields to a pacific touch.

Squares divided once are now at ease
Fitfully. England looks up in Winter
Suggesting nowhere an enduring place.
We do not ask that, we but ask to wander,
With tacit lack of absolutes. A chanter
In the cold wood sets the mind to ponder

On its own value and the worth of those
Collected trees which kneel into the light,
The falling light which has ways to disclose
The secrets hoarded for a frosty night.
We drift into the dark where each dream goes
With unexpected order. What insight
Will shift in sleep towards us? No one knows.

Lent and Spring

It has come fast, another Lent,
Hard on the thaw. The Winter went
Suddenly. Few were prepared
For the spilt sun, or singing bird.

The elms are killed. None can be saved,
And every meadow looks bereaved,
Ash on the brow, sin in the mind.
Our spirits burn low, eyes are blind.

But Lent is in the Spring, maybe,
That grace should burst out naturally,
That we may learn from birds and flowers
That we depend on one God's powers,

A God, however, who needs us.
What better motive can we use
To make ourselves at one with these
Blossom-waiting apple trees?

What better way to tell again
The Eden story and its pain?
But there's a death that felled the world.
A God died once. Spring air was cold

But strong belief affirms that this
God-man rose up, kept promises.
O Christ upon a flowering tree,
Be your own Spring, blossom with me.

A Way to a Creed

Mine is a hard creed and often is at odds
With my mercury nature. It informs my mind,
Tells of truths apparent to the blind
But not to me. I am afraid of Gods,
And yet when a line sings through me and I find

A poem telling me what I did not know
Before about myself or my character
I need to thank, for it's then I find myself near
A presence in the universe. I go
About with a new hope and without fear.

So I come into a childhood creed again,
Come to it like the prodigal son and am
Welcomed with understanding, as if there were some
God who, yes, needs me in a daily pain.
He, like me, is also coming home.

Always that dark cross throws its shadow on me
And I am often in the garden where
Christ came so often to the brink of despair.
It is, I think, in my own poetry
I meet my God. He's a familiar there.

CELEBRATIONS AND ELEGIES

1982

A Kind of Catalogue

Item, a cloud, and how it changes shape,
Now a pink balloon, then a white shift
From a Victorian doll. The forms won't keep
One pattern long. Item, a flow of wind
Carrying dust and paper, gathering up

Rose petals. Item, a command of sun
Subtly presented on a lifted face,
A shaft of light on leaves, darkness undone
And packed away. Item, limbs moved with grace,
Turning the air aside. Item, my own

Observations, now *Lot This, Lot That*
Ready for an unseen auctioneer.
The bidders are half-conscious choices met
To haggle. Signs are made, sometimes I hear
My whisper bidding for *Lot This, Lot That.*

Rescued

These are the many but they must be praised.
They have known dark valleys but have raised
Their eyes to rings of stars. They have climbed up
Hillsides and cliffs and felt the vertigo
Of height but have gone on, not looked below
But watched the sky and rested at the top.

Do not imagine these have never been
In *cul de sacs* of near-despair and seen
Death as desirable. They have and they
Have turned away from it. It is good luck
Simply to be and these have turned their back
On the dark stranger who stands in the way

Of life, the breath of it, its primal power
Settled in us, with each one given our
Specific strength. That stranger's had his toll
Of many lost. Some were nearly so
But brought back by great mercy. This I know
For I gave up but felt a great power pull

Me back and now I see why and am glad,
Also ashamed. Call that power God,
As I do, call it fortune. I have found
Some use in all those shadows. They have told
Me of the terror that makes dying bold
But now I hear its soft retreating sound.

Recovering from a Death

We are back with our disorders again.
Last year's death has moved into the dark,
For with a real death the shadows drain
Away. All is exact and pure and stark.
    Fear of death has been

Among us since the final mourning seeped
Away. So fear, it seems, is healthy. We
Creep, stride, manoeuvre, once again are kept
Afraid. I think we miss the dignity
    Of mourning. We were stripped

Of all pretence. Love showed its proper size,
Small circumstances drifted quietly off.
Not to mourn can be a loss. We prize
A perfect grief, an almost selfless love
    And wide, defenceless eyes.

Is it Dual-Natured?

Is it dual-natured to be so alive
Sometimes that your flesh seems far too small
To contain the power of the sun, or how stars thrive,

But then to be diminished, become a small
Dark of yourself, yourself your hiding place
Where you converse with shadows which are tall

Or listen to low echoes with no grace
Of lyric joy or calm? I do not feel
Divided deep. Sometimes, the sense of the place

Where I am most light and eager can make me thrill
To the planet's course. I am pulled, or do
I draw myself up, into the sun's overspill?

One or other. It only matters I know
What levitation would be and am grateful to learn
What's instinctive to birds is what makes the wind blow.

I will risk all extremes. I will flounder, will stumble, will burn.

EXTENDING THE TERRITORY

1985

The Child's Story

When I was small and they talked about love I laughed
But I ran away and I hid in a tall tree
Or I lay in asparagus beds
But I still listened.
The blue dome sang with the wildest birds
And the new sun sang in the idle noon
But then I heard love, love, rung from the steeples, each belfry,
And I was afraid and I watched the cypress trees
Join the deciduous chestnuts and oaks in a crowd of shadows
And then I shivered and ran and ran to the tall
White house with the green shutters and dark red door
And I cried 'Let me in even if you must love me'
And they came and lifted me up and told me the name
Of the near and the far stars,
And so my first love was.

Clarify

Clarify me, please,
God of the galaxies,
Make me a meteor,
Or else a metaphor

So lively that it grows
Beyond its likeness and
Stands on its own, a land
That nobody can lose.

God, give me liberty
But not so much that I
See you on Calvary,
Nailed to the wood by me.

Love in Three Movements

Comings
In moonlight or in sunlight, the immediate
Heat of Summer laying on the leaves
Hot hands. A little breeze, a wisp of breath
Cools the purpose of the heyday noon.

Goings
In Winter or in Autumn when nostalgia
Cancels the present, stops the clocks, endures
In our imaginations of a better,
A standing-still world, stable universe.

Retreats
As bonfire smoke hides figures in the streets.
The spirit's urgency –
How it will exercise our passions, put
Power not ours on our blunt purposes.
The spirit moves inquiring fingers, lips
Touching, pressing, then the mind asks questions,
Gives an order. How our spirits threaten
The bodies' movements they intend to sweeten.

The Way of Words and Language

When you are lost
Even near home, when you feel
The tide turning, a strange sea under you
And you are a pale, rubbed pebble, a sea ghost,

When you have lost
All the highways and every dimming signpost
And the sea is far away and the moon hidden
And your watch has stopped and you have no compass
And feel to yourself like a ghost,

All this later will seem your best
Time for there will be future and memory and the tossed
Tide. Morning will come up and you will open your eyes
And see in the mirror a ghost.

But day will take you and the dawn uncover
The ribbed sand foot by foot and the first light
Will stretch over the grey water and you will know
It is no longer night

But still a time of silence and light like a shielded lamp.
Then you will shake off dreams and recover
What you know is yourself still but changed
And the new sun will come up and pass over
Your hands, your arms, your face and you will discover
A world that the night has rearranged.

Let this time be. Let the present stay. Do not
Look back. Do not look forward. Let thought
Idle from dream into daylight, and watch, then, the coast
Climb out to dark, to grey, and then to chalk-white
Cliffs till the grey sea goes blue
And then indeed you

Are found and safe at last
And all your thought will grow
And you will unreel it, a silk thread, a long-
Travelling, moving-everywhere line
And it will gradually, as you relax it, become a song
And you will not say 'That is mine'.

Song of Time

Deliver time and let it go
Under wild clouds and passive moon.
Once it was fast, now it is slow.
I loose my hours beneath the sun,
Brisk minutes ebb and flow.

Time is elemental, all
We make in speech and action, yet
Time itself can have a fall
When heart and mind have no regret
And love is how you feel.

O let us dance with time and turn
It to a friend, a willing one.
In time we grow, through time we learn
The visitations of the sun
And ardour of the moon.

Time is not clocks but moves within
The discourse of the learned heart.
It is the way our lives begin.
O leaving time behind's an art
Ahead and now and then.

Water Music

What I looked for was a place where water
Flowed continually. It could come
In rapids, over rocks in great falls and
Arrive at stillness far below. I watched
The hidden power. And then I went to rivers,
The source and mouth, the place where estuaries
Were the last, slow-moving waters and
The sea lay not far off continually
Making her music,
Loud gulls interrupting.
At first I only listened to her music,
Slow movements first, the held-back waves
With all their force to rear and roar and stretch
Over the waiting sand. Sea music is
What quiets my spirit. I would like my death
To come as rivers turn, as sea commands.
Let my last journey be to sounds of water.

TRIBUTES

1989

Against the Dark

I have lived in a time of opulent grief,
    In a place also of powers
Where self-indulgence can break your purchase on life
    But now I inhabit hours

Of careful joy and rousing gratitude.
    My spirit has learnt to play
And I have willed away the darker mood
    And now I want to say

That verse is hostile to shadows and casts you out
    When you have mourned too long.
Images always rise from the root of light
    And I must make my song

Truthful, yes, obstinate too and yet
    Open to love that takes
Language by the hand and ignores regret
    And also our heartbreaks.

Words use me. Time is a metronome
    I must keep in mind always.
Nobody really knows where poems come from
    But I believe they must praise

Even when grief is threatening, even when hope
    Seems as far as the furthest star.
Poetry uses me, I am its willing scope
    And proud practitioner.

Beginning

It is to be found halfway between sleep and waking –
A starting point, a recognition, beginning.
Think of the clouds on this planet lifted away
And the stars snapped off and the day tremendously breaking
And everything clear and absolute, the good morning
Striking the note of the day.

So it was and so it is always and still
Whether you notice or not. Forget that you are
Eyes, nose, ears but attend. So much must go on
Daily and hourly. Wait for the morning to fill
With cockcrow and petals unfolding, the round planet's power
Held in the hands of the sun.

And somewhere around are presences, always have been,
Whose hands remove clouds, whose fingers prise open the sun.
Watch, learn the craft of beginning and seeing the world
Disclose itself. Take this down to a small thing, a keen
Whisper of wind, the sound of the cock or your own
Story that waits to be told.

I stood at a window once. I was four or five
And I watched the sun open the garden and spread out the grass
And heard the far choir of some blackbirds and watched blue
                                        flowers rise.
This was the first day for me, the planet alive,
And I watched the stars' shadows grow faint and finally pass
And I could not believe my eyes.

TIMES AND SEASONS

1992

from *For My Mother*

VIII   Let Me Learn

Let me learn from you now
    Or is it too late?
The North wind starts to sough,
    Coal shifts in the grate.

Once in a white and high
    Nursery we played as if
The ceiling were the sky,
    Each hour all life.

You and my father came
    After a dance
Bringing bright favours home.
    It still enchants

To think of you young as then.
    Your face never was
Wrinkled with lines even when
    Death took its place

Within you, beside you, all
    About. I was dry
With sorrow but tears do fall
    Now. You don't die

Over and over but are
    Installed beside
The pile of books laid here,
    The lamplight wide.

You read in bed, I feel
　　Your heart stirring in mine
And everything starts to heal.
　　What a delicate line

Death writes when love was the drift
　　Of a life like yours.
At all my fears you laughed
　　And cast out their force.

There will be no wind tonight,
　　No angry words
And at dawn a strong light
　　And chattering birds.

Poems, praise, prayer –
　　In these I find
Your gentle atmosphere,
　　Your steady mind.

The Smell of Chrysanthemums

The chestnut leaves are toasted. Conkers spill
Upon the pavements. Gold is vying with
Yellow, ochre, brown. There is a feel
Of dyings and departures. Smoky breath
    Rises and I know how Winter comes
    When I can smell the rich chrysanthemums.

It is so poignant and it makes me mourn
For what? The going year? The sun's eclipse?
All these and more. I see the dead leaves burn
And everywhere the Summer lies in heaps.
    I close my eyes and feel how Winter comes
    With acrid incense of chrysanthemums.

I shall not go to school again and yet
There's an old sadness that disturbs me most.
The nights come early; every bold sunset
Tells me that Autumn soon will be a ghost,
    But I know best how Winter always comes
    In the wide scent of strong chrysanthemums.

In Green Times

Let the blossom blow back to the tree,
Let the wind be lost in silences,
Let my childhood wake again round me,
    Its sweets and violences.

Out of that white nursery I came
Into the garden green to wade in deep.
Quiet broke with calling of my name
    I acted half-asleep.

I listened to the bees. I felt the grass
Touch me softly. I would watch the sun
And every truant cloud that had to pass.
    I was at peace alone.

Nature was my shelter. All the berries
Plumped and showed their shining. I was there
In what could be a Summer's dream. Time's worries
    Found no foothold near.

And nor did mine. Perspectives happened later.
All my world was flat and full of green.
Mountains face me. Rivers mirror me,
I am all aware and frightened too
But I can't turn back pages now to see
    What once was green and true.

A Litany for Contrition

Dew on snowdrop
                weep for me
Rain in a rose
                cleanse my heart,
Bud of crocus
                candle me to
Contrition. Far stars
                shine from your great
Heights, and burn my faults away.

Half-moon emerging
                from a cloud
Strengthen my spirit.
                All Spring flowers,
More each day,
                in this night now
Give me a scent of our sweet powers.

A shower of rain
                wash me clean,
Let my spirit glow
                for I have seen
The terrible depth
                of dark in me.
Christ, you alone
                can cure jealousy.

First Confession

So long ago and yet it taunts me still,
That First Confession. I was only seven
When I first knelt by that impersonal grille
And poured my little sins out one by one.
I never felt near God or any Heaven.
It was my thefts which made all that undone

Or never started. Certainly the priest
Was not unkind though he told me I must
Return those things. I think my childhood ceased
Upon that day. My spirit had been light
And happy for six years. I lost my trust
And learnt a little of the spirit's night.

From that day on this healing sacrament
Was hurting for me. No one's fault, it's true,
And yet I think the child's right element
Of joy should not be risked so early but
Left till youth sends doubt and darkness through
Flesh and soul and childhood's door slams shut.

Star-Gazing

Give it a name. It is still there,
One on its own, another star
    Which is not yours and is not mine.

And yet we need to find a name,
To lay indeed a kind of claim,
    A beauty wrought to our design.

But we are wrong. We don't possess
The stars. Our words make them grow less
    As we waylay them to define.

They shine a love. Another one
Is there tonight. The Summer sun
    Left the horizon's steady line.

Think, there are more than we can count,
Star after star, O such amount,
    Each seems to flicker out a sign,

To hand a message. It is this:
'We are much further than you guess
    And brighter too. Yes, we combine

Distance and light to give a show
Like fireworks which retain their glow,
    We keep a rich unmeasured shine.'

The voices pause. I look again,
The sky is pouring silver rain
    Which could be yours and might be mine.

The Way They Live Now

You make love and you live together now
Where we were shy and made love by degrees.
By kiss and invitation we learnt how
Our love was growing. You know few of these

Tokens and little gifts, the gaze of eye
To eye, the hand shared with another hand.
You know of few frustrations, seldom cry
With passion's stress, yet do you understand

The little gestures that would mean so much,
The surging hope to be asked to a dance?
You take the whole of love. We lived by touch

And doubt and by the purposes of chance
And yet I think our slow ways carried much
That you have missed – the guess, the wish, the glance.

FAMILIAR SPIRITS

1994

It is Not True?

It comes to me at midnight it is true
We don't believe in death. It can't be so –
Or not for those we know as me and you.

It is a state, a happening, an event
For those who're strangers to us. Death is meant
For others. In newspapers in dark print

We read of great ones going. We think of
The fact a moment, then turn back to love
And care and all the ways that we must move

To work, to play, while death goes on elsewhere.
It is a message carried through the air,
Something that happened when we were not there.

But wait, a day arrives when someone close
Is taken ill and dies. We feel the loss
And thoughts of our own deaths return to us.

My mother died two years ago today.
I often think of questions I could say
That only she could answer. She's away

But where and how? O love, we quarrel and
Neither will speak. Then one puts out a hand
The other takes. We start to understand

Our final goings and we are afraid
And I, not you, believe we are not made
To go forever. When we often said

Death is not true, I think we were in part
Precisely right. When we make works of art
We think they'll last. O when did mankind start

To think of death as somehow to begin
Our lives a different way, to start again
And live life flawlessly? Our minds move in

Countries untried but waiting for us. Love
Conjures up lands which death knows nothing of
And forevers are convincing proof,

And hint at lastings. Love goes further still,
Suggesting we have spirits death can't kill.
O love I am afraid of this as well.

Almost

It almost was not. That is what I say
About this minute coloured by the sea,
About this chestnut losing its huge hands
About the boys who pick the polished conkers.
This almost was not now and setting sun
In pink surrenders, scarlet streaks foretelling
Good weather certainly. Now,
I celebrate the clothing of all these,
Their singing and their colour and this now
We stand in peacefully as night intrudes
In kind dark dusk. O celebrate with me.

from *The Modes of Love*

Married Love

A sonnet for D. and A.

They do not use the words of passion now
But they speak tender nicknames now and then.
They are familiar yet they both know how
Precious love always is and so they mean

Each word that tells of sharing. They see much
Of partings and divorce and know the worth
Of private languages and gentle touch.
Marriage makes them monarchs of the earth.

I knew a couple whom I praised for this.
They smiled and said, 'We have our quarrels though,
You must not think that everything is bliss.'

But as they spoke these words they both looked so
Compassionate, they proved that marriage is
A marvel which can somehow daily grow.

IN THE MEANTIME

1996

The Spirit's Power

All the sheen and cut, the tied, the true
Of almost anything I praise and watch.
I clap my hands when Nature shows her due
Respect for us but how does spirit go

On? Strip off each trying sense, think how
The spirit works. It has its own success
As I think hard and leave the here and now.
My spirit is the way that I seek grace

And how it corresponds with what I do.
The flesh creeps slowly offering dubious powers.
I will five senses off but they won't go

For long. I have known rare and kindly hours
That leap from love and then I think of you
As I last saw you, gathering wild flowers.

PRAISES

1998

Walking in the Dark

In a dark mood I wandered at night-time,
Most people were in bed, some lights still shone.
In the far distance trains made happy sounds,
A going off with jubilation. I
      Tried to think of them,
       In childhood distant trains
       Were a good lullaby.
But now I was grown-up and wandered looking ... for what?
I did not know and yet I felt my spirit
Stirring with some glad power.
Between a dream and a nightmare I had come
To this strange city not on any map
That I'd been shown at school
And yet I knew I had to take quiet steps
Even as I felt afraid of crossing
Almost every street. What fear was this?
Where did it come from? Why
Had it made me think
I must put on a jacket and go out?
The season was so vague, the moon was half
But not a star was there for me to look at,
Not a human being anywhere
Could join this search whose goal I did not know.
The God whom I had always prayed to still
Existed but he seemed too far away
To give a blessing or explain why I
Had to walk upon what was perhaps
A pilgrimage though there was not a sign

In air, on ground, close to the moon, to say
I must know dark and carry it about.
Dear God, this was a doubt about a doubt.

Round and Round

The children asked 'Where is the end of the world?'
And we started telling them about horizons
And how the sun does not really go down
As it seems to us to be doing.

They were all frowning and obviously didn't believe us.
We looked at each other and wordlessly agreed
That scientific speeches were useless and so
After a fairly long pause
We told them all the ancient stories
About the sun moving around the world
And rising and setting over and over again.
They listened, did not speak, but they stopped frowning.
When we said, 'Of course that isn't quite true',
They put their hands over their ears and ran out
Letting what we call knowledge lag behind them.

Praises

I praise those things I always take for granted: –
The tap my sister turns on for my bath
Every time I stay, the safety pin –
And who invented it? I do not know –
The comb, the piece of soap, a shoe, its shine,
The name tape and the string, a leather purse –
How they all flock as I recall them now,
And Now I also praise with all it holds
Of nudges, hand-shakes, playing trains with children.
There is no end until I'm tired and think
Of craftsmen everywhere … O I forgot,
Cushions, napkins, stoves and cubes of ice.
All the world is praise or else is war.
Tonight the moon is almost half in shape,
'Tomorrow will be hot' say weathermen.
I praise the yawning kind of sleep that's coming,
And where the spirit goes, the sheet, the pillow …

TIMELY ISSUES

2001

The Story

I knew that it lay about me,
I knew that the story I had to live was near
But fenced off. Only I
Could find the entrance, and not by straining and fighting
But only, always, by

Being prepared for the great surrender, the huge
Advance and appearance. Nothing to do with fear
Was this. I only had
To let the four seasons march in order ahead,
To watch the sky changing and meeting the sea.
This was the way I had to let things happen,
To let the world appear
In all its golden finish and lucky end.
I watched the door of morning start to open,
I simply put out my hand.

Rage of the Moon

Rest, heavy head, on the wood
    Of the good, old desk-stand.
Dreams must be understood
    And the right hand

Feels for purchase upon
    A fine, old, open page
Of writing lit by the moon
    And its light rage.

Assurance

My love, I hold you in imagination,
    Either mine or yours,
And it is stronger than remembered passion.
It uses memory with all its force.

O and the clocks go silent, time departs,
    Now is forever here.
How delicate yet strong are our two hearts,
Mine beats for you now almost everywhere.

Only when my world is rent with storm,
    Threatened by sadness or
Overcome by black words which can come
And threaten me with the inner, hideous war,

Only then, I've lost you – O but fast
    A little flash of sun,
A hurrying memory returns you blessed
And our great love is stalwartly at one.

Song in November 2000

Count within me your minutes, hours,
    The turned tide of the sea,
Count me among your Summer flowers
    And Winter's leaf-bare tree.
Count me by every bell which rings,
    By every clock which ticks.
Count me in all your time-bound things
    And candles' blackened wicks.

Whatever loss still hurts for you
    Shed tears until your grief
Ends the story that is true,
    The pattern of your life.
Even if love should end you must
    Let it and be free.
Time blows away our fickle dust
    But, in arched memory,

Stories by stories still are told
    And no one tires of these,
They change to myths when they are old
    And show the shape of peace.
Count every death as ended war
    Which has its minstrelsy.
If you have ever loved before,
    Your book of memory

Shows page on page which you may turn
    And read or let alone.
Doing either you can learn
    That birth and death are one.
We write the chapters of our lives
    By good or evil will
And page by page each one survives
    While someone reads them still.

Now is the turn of music to
   Choose trumpets, strings or drum.
They will assist each grief to go,
   Fresh happiness to come.
Music takes memory and lets
   Theme and use and range
Be heard in every note which fits
   And rings the needed change.

Turn the score of melody,
   Slowly let silence tell
The eager tale of memory
   That gives life yet stays still.

Assurance Beyond Midnight

Wisdom or music come in these small hours,
Their clarities combine and I allow
Myself almost to rest in their good powers.

But it's a lively rest that I know now,
Compulsions cease and everything around
Fits in a meaning though I don't know how.

I only know rich purpose with a sound
Of settlements suggests itself and I
Listen for theme and arguments, the ground

Of God's great Being. Stars are very high,
The moon is full, a warm September makes
Seasons a mood here though I don't know why.

But I know well that now my spirit wakes
And is assured. Imagination is
Rich. Helped out of sickness and heartbreaks

I feel in touch with everything that's peace
And later on there will arrive with dawn
A bold assurance and a synthesis

Of what waits for me not much further on,
But near enough to tell me faith is bold
And proves itself in all that has been done

To me and for me in a golden world.

Afterword

In one sense, Elizabeth Jennings's literary career was exemplary. Over the course of fifty years she authored and edited forty-eight books, encompassing poetry, literary criticism and theology, and became one of the most widely anthologised and bestselling poets of the second half of the twentieth century. Her early poetry collections won substantial prizes, granting her the opportunity of European travel, which brought new spiritual and formal dimensions and a lyric openness to her work. Her first *Collected Poems*, published in 1987, won the W.H. Smith Literary Award, and through the 1980s and '90s her poems were required reading on the English A-Level syllabus. On 29 October 1992 she attended a ceremony at Buckingham Palace where she was appointed CBE for services to literature. ('That was quite interesting,' she reflected in a subsequent interview; 'I got a medal and I even had to walk backwards.') Following her death in 2001, the City Council in Oxford, where she had spent most of her life, named a street after her: Elizabeth Jennings Way.

Alongside these outward markers of success, Jennings's career was shaped by intense suffering: the torture of religious guilt and doubt; the enduring sense of isolation that resulted from unconsummated and unrequited love; sustained bouts of physical and mental illness; long-term financial hardship. These experiences fed into her work, obliquely and directly. She wrote through them, and wrote prolifically, not (as interviewers liked to suggest) in an attempt to heal, but because she felt that writing poetry was 'the one thing I *can* do'. Among her archived papers, which are scattered across several US institutions (Jennings sold them off piecemeal to generate income in her later years), are more than 30,000 unpublished poems, manuscript fragments and autobiographical writings.

Jennings was born on 18 July 1926, the second daughter of a physician and his 'gentle' wife, and spent her first six years in Boston, Lincolnshire, within walking distance of the sea. South of the Lincolnshire Wolds, the landscape that borders the eastern coastline is notoriously flat, yielding huge skies. Stars were a major feature of her early sensory world, and appear frequently in her poems both as visual phenomena (observable radiances) and as metaphors for transcendent powers and a celestial order. 'Something of me is out in the dark landscape', she writes in 'In the Night', recognising early on the difficulty of reconciling this elemental aspect of the self, attuned to the world outside, with the mind, whose thoughts 'divide / me from my object'. In the later poem 'Star-Gazing', the stars' 'distance and light' represent the simultaneous impossibility of romantic possession and the enduring beauty (and pathos) of the unattainable love object – a recurring theme in her work.

Jennings looked back on her early years as a rural idyll, a time of perfect innocence, 'when our hearts were our own privilege' and experience was characterised by 'that quick openness, that sense of peace' that adolescence and adulthood would destroy ('Never to See'). In her later books part of her poetic project is to recover, and awaken in her readers, the sense of childlike wonder and acuity of sensory perception she recalls in poems such as 'Beginning' and 'In Green Times', when:

> Nature was my shelter. All the berries
> Plumped and showed their shining. I was there
> In what could be a Summer's dream. Time's worries
> Found no foothold near.

When the family relocated to north Oxford in 1932, Jennings attended a Catholic school, which instilled in her a persistent sense of guilt and a deep fear of the wrathful, Old Testament God who she learnt was waiting to punish her for her sins. At seven she underwent her first Confession – a damaging experience. 'I think my childhood ceased / Upon that day', she reflected six decades later, in *Times and Seasons*. In the early poem 'Answers' the speaker recounts her strategies for dealing with the 'big questions' and 'huge abstractions' that underpinned religious doubt and existential unease: 'Small things I handled and caressed and loved. / I let the stars assume the whole of night.' Such strategies proved inadequate; the poem hinges, as so many of Jennings's poems do, on 'but', and the speaker is left floundering, futilely trying to secure 'protection of my spirit' against the 'great conclusions coming near'. Throughout her subsequent childhood and adolescent years she bore the wounds (later the scars) of doubt, guilt and psychological and sexual repression – though she always enjoyed the Mass, with its rituals and music, its incitements to exaltation and its focus on transformation.

Her poetic awakening came at age thirteen when she was a pupil at the (non-Catholic) Oxford High School. Reading 'Lepanto', G.K. Chesterton's rousing poem about the triumph of Christian Europe over its non-Christian enemies, in class yielded her first experience of 'the curious mixture of excitement and exaltation' that she subsequently claimed to be looking for in her encounters with poetry. When she started writing her own poems as a teenager, her mother provided stamps and envelopes so that she could submit them to magazines. Her first significant publication came in her early twenties, shortly after she completed her English literature degree at St Anne's College in Oxford. While enrolled as a probationer B. Litt. student in 1947–48, she met Kingsley Amis, who printed several of her poems in *Oxford Poetry*, effectively launching her onto the Oxford literary scene. Over the next few years, while working as Assistant Librarian at Oxford City Library, Jennings found herself part of an enthusiastic community of poets, the younger members of which cast her as a role model, dubbing themselves 'Elizabethans'.

Following publication of a pamphlet (the first in the Fantasy Press's numbered pamphlet series) in 1952, Jennings's debut collection, *Poems*, came out in 1953 and was awarded an Arts Council Prize for the best first book of poetry published in the previous two years. *Poems* is striking for the confidence and technical virtuosity with which Jennings constructs philosophical conceits out of concrete imagery. Already her signature motifs – stars, light, architecture, water, music, bells – are in evidence, acting as worldly anchors for the poems' abstract arguments about the obscuring nature of thought. In poems such as 'Bell-Ringer', 'The Climbers' and 'Fishermen' it is through physical and sensual activity that people move towards a state of spiritual awakening and transcendence.

This direct and ambitious engagement with questions of epistemology and ontology – of the irresolvable tension, or gap, between appearances and reality, and between the intellect and the emotions – also dominated Jennings's second collection, *A Way of Looking* (1955), which won her a Somerset Maugham Award in 1956. This was a turning point in her life and in her writing. With the £400 prize money she travelled to Italy, where she encountered (especially in Rome) a model of lived religion and embodied faith of which she could make sense. For the first time, she later remarked, 'spirit and flesh stopped battling and made peace with each other'. Life, ritual and art became one channel.

The poems she wrote during this time, which were published in her third collection, *A Sense of the World* (1958), proceed from the world rather than from abstract considerations. A few embrace free verse; in others the tight rhyme schemes and stanzaic structures that dominate her first two collections relax into blank verse. 'Fountain' is a breakthrough poem, addressed directly to the reader, inviting us to share in the visionary experience communicated through the poem's conversational tones:

> And then step closer,
> Imagine rivers you might indeed embark on,
> Waterfalls where you could
> Silence an afternoon by staring but never
> See the same tumult twice.
> Yes come out of the narrow street and enter
> The full piazza. Come where the noise compels.
> Statues are bowing down to the breaking air.

Evoking a specific place and time through sensory details, the poem transcends its physical context, transporting us to the shared vista of 'some perpetual stream', into which our ancestors might once also have gazed in 'deepest wonder'. The fountain, with its simultaneous 'energy' and 'taming' quality, becomes a touchstone for universal human experience, and the poem builds to the earned second-person plural ('we') that would later distinguish Jennings's work from the confessional tones of her contemporaries. 'Letter from Assisi' broadens the territory in a different way, achieving an individual stance in which the speaker's delicate sensibilities are laid bare and weighed against the broader forces of history and nationhood:

> Now on this road, looking up to the hill
> Where the town looks severe and seems to say
> There is no softness here, no sensual joy,

Close by the flowers that fling me back to England –
The bleeding poppy and the dusty vetch
And all blue flowers reflecting back the sky –
It is not peace I feel but some nostalgia,
So that a hand which draws a shutter back,
An eye which warms as it observes a child,
Hurt me with homesickness.

Other notable Jennings characteristics that emerge in *A Sense of the World* are a clarity and coherence of place and image (as in, for example, 'Absence' and 'A Roman Window'); the curious way she has of balancing the personal and the symbolic, so that a poem is held flickering between candour and metaphor, or lyricism and parable, without committing fully to either mode (as in 'Choices', 'Hurt', 'I Feel' and 'The Child's Story'); and the ability to handle stark oppositions – complexity and clarity, abstracts and concretes, interiors and exteriors, isolation and communal feeling – within tight formal structures (as in the astonishing poem 'A Fear').

Changed by her experience of travel, Jennings resolved to give up her employment at the library and become a full-time writer. Yet the offer of a new job as a manuscript reader at Chatto & Windus intervened, luring her temporarily to London. From October 1958 to the summer of 1960 she juggled employment, relationships (including a failed engagement), an active social life, poetry writing and literary-critical projects with determination and aplomb. A colleague at Chatto & Windus arranged for her to have tea with T.S. Eliot, who advised her on which writers she should read for her critical study of mystics and mystical poets, *Every Changing Shape* (one of five books she would go on to publish in 1961). *A Song for a Birth or a Death*, her fourth collection of poems, was the Poetry Book Society's Summer Choice for 1961, and it is unsurprising that she achieved popularity with these poems, which circle around difficult questions of family ties, romantic love and religious experience. The startling combination of sensory detail and allegorical motifs in the title poem, and of frankness and formality in 'My Grandmother', constitute two of the high points in her oeuvre.

While Jennings successfully consolidated her literary reputation during these years, the rate and intensity of her work proved unsustainable. Months of physical pain and illness culminated in surgery on her gallbladder and a related ulcer, necessitating a move back to the family home in Oxford. The added complication that her parents were simultaneously planning to relocate permanently to the south coast of England left Jennings fearful, depressed and, on three occasions, suicidal. Characteristically, she was still writing. The poems in *Recoveries* (1964) and *The Mind Has Mountains* (1966) are more than a record of individual suffering: their stance is outward facing; their speakers search compassionately for commonalities of experience, moving steadfastly towards an articulation of the implacable boundaries between illness and health, between the restrictive interiors of the hospital and the vigorous world beyond. Despite the context of their composition, these poems evince a clarity of perception and insight that enables their speakers to transcend (rather than simply document) their situations, and to discover a sense of community that sustains them through the worst of times. 'Measured off a space / There is a world where things run calm and true – / But not for us', the speaker calmly acknowledges in 'Madness' – a poem Jennings did not choose for her 1979 *Selected Poems*, but which I have included here for its achievement of the communal perspective, the earned 'we', which unites the patients in the hospital even as it divides them from the world outside. Likewise 'Attempted Suicides', in which the language is characteristically devoid of ornament, and empathy expands from the simple, physical details and off-kilter imagery: 'Hands are muslin / Babies look eatable. / [...] Now we touch ourselves and feel strange.'

As Jennings's first biographer, Dana Greene, has suggested: 'Jennings's institutionalization was a pivotal experience in her life, one formative of her future, much as her time in Rome had been. Although life in the Warneford [Hospital] nearly destroyed her, it brought with it an increased compassion for all those who suffered and were misunderstood. This new sensitivity would find its way into her poetry. It also deepened her religious experience.' Her subsequent poetry collections were powered by a combination of sensitivity to the pains and joys of worldly experience, and faith in the existence of a divine harmony that could occasionally be glimpsed or felt through the proxies of Christian ritual, art and music and the energies of the seasons. *Moments of Grace* (1979) is perhaps the best collection from Jennings's middle period – the one in which she recovers the lyrical power and intellectual clarity first established in *A Sense of the World*. In poems such as 'Into the Hour', 'Forgiveness' and 'Thought and Feeling' she manages to bring theology and worldliness into union. Doubt and assurance, suffering and acceptance, coexist; the poems seem to evolve a set of practical values, derived from tender observations, and they grant permission to grief even as they find a way forward via sensory experience:

> I need not speak though everyone I pass
> Stares at me kindly. I would put my hand
> Into their hands. Now I have lost my loss
>
> In some way I may later understand.
> I hear the singing of the Summer grass
> And love, I find, has no considered end [...]

The old themes – love, loss, illness, the seasons – find new expression, and a new flexibility in the relaxed enjambments and delicate rhymes.

While Jennings continued to frustrate reviewers with her mixture of linguistic freshness and repetitive subject matter, naïve sentimentality and intellectual flair, her *Selected Poems*, published in 1979, sold out in two weeks and went on to sell 50,000 copies, and a new *Collected Poems*, published in 1985, sold in excess of 35,000 copies. Throughout the 1970s and '80s her work was widely anthologised and she received several significant bursaries, which she needed. Living alone in Oxford, she spent her days in cafes, writing and striking up conversations with regulars and newcomers alike. In the evenings she spent time at friends' houses or retired to her modest accommodation to read and write, often staying up into the early hours and working in bed with a notebook on her knees.

Despite her sustained productivity, and her large and committed following among the poetry-reading public, her finances remained precarious. During the 1990s she unhappily occupied a series of inadequate and temporary lodgings, separated from her treasured possessions (collections of music boxes, dolls' houses and other bric-a-brac), which had to be kept in storage. In 1997 she received a Hamlyn Foundation Award, given to help artists overcome disadvantages and realise their potential; this amounted to £15,000, which was more than Jennings had earned in any previous year. As her health gradually failed she focused, as well as on poetry, on writing a long essay about Gerard Manley Hopkins, a poet who had always been central to her religion and to her work. She did not finish it, nor did she live to see her final collection of poems, *Timely Issues*, into print. Following her death on 26 October 2001, all the major newspapers ran obituaries, celebrating her unique contribution to the poetic landscape of the previous half-century.

It is difficult to decide where the oeuvre of a poet as popular, prolific and inconsistent as Elizabeth Jennings sits within the literary canon. As numerous critics have pointed out, she wrote too much. Her published books were for the most part constructed by her editors, with each serviceable poem having to be plucked from the vast tangles of manuscript material that she periodically handed over. Though her poetic trajectory 'from an essentially thinking poet to a feeling and suffering poet', as Michael Schmidt has described it, can be broadly traced through her published works, she was neither a poet of her time nor a poet writing against her time. Her overarching concern was transcendence: an anachronistic spiritual quest, which rendered her work unfashionable and out of place in a secular, sceptical and postmodern age.

Jennings emerged from the post-war period as a member by default of a generation of poets who broadly recognised the necessity of finding a new tone to replace the romantic excesses that had dominated much of the poetry of the 1940s. In the mid-1950s her name was invoked in conjunction with 'the Movement' – a motley assemblage of poets including John Holloway, Philip Larkin, Thom Gunn, Kingsley Amis, D.J. Enright, Donald Davie and John Wain, whose early work Robert Conquest had 'marshalled together' (Jennings thought) into the first of his *New Lines* anthologies, published in 1956. Jennings was the only Christian among them, a distinction she believed fundamentally separated her poetics from theirs. As she later observed (in *Poetry To-day*), the main qualities these poets shared were 'clarity, honesty and formal perfection – qualities which we expect to find in all worthwhile poetry'. While she considered 'this clarity, accessibility and tact' to be 'really valuable qualities which have emerged from the Movement', it was clear to her and others that by the end of the decade even those Movementeers who had appeared superficially to share an intellectual or technical project were each 'developing away from the group' in various ways.

While Jennings can occasionally be seen to inhabit Larkinesque territory (as in, for example, 'Family Affairs'), her approach is always more tender and delicate than Larkin's; while both poets deal in pathos and sadness, Jennings (even in her angry moments) is never snide. Similarities can be traced in their theorising about poetry, with each arguing on different occasions for the necessary self-sufficiency of the poem: 'As a guiding principle I believe that every poem must be its own sole freshly-created universe,' Larkin stated; 'But poetry must change and make / The world seem new in each design', Jennings writes in 'Considerations'. Whether she resisted, or was incapable of, the calm ironies characteristic of Larkin's poetry, she perceived in his best work (citing 'Church Going' and 'Reasons for Attendance') that, despite his claims to the contrary, his poems 'not only can but actually want to enter the world of big emotions and profound human experiences'.

Her comments on other poets are always illuminating. From the previous generation she identified Louis MacNeice as 'the most satisfying and accessible of the thirties poets', on the basis that 'his verse is always primarily *communication*; MacNeice is a poet talking not to himself but to others'. Echoes of MacNeice – notably his nostalgic engagement with the tropes of childhood in poems such as 'Trains in the Distance' and 'When We Were Children', and the flexible rhythms he evolved through *Autumn Journal* – can be heard in Jennings's work. In her introductory note to *A Way of Looking* (written for the Poetry Book Society's *Bulletin* magazine), she identifies Yeats, Edwin Muir and Wallace Stevens as 'the modern poets whom I most admire' and whom she considers influences not in the way of technique but because 'they have acted as liberators, have shown me the most direct way into my own world'.

For her primary influences, however, she turned to the religious poets of the seventeenth century – in particular to George Herbert, Thomas Traherne and Henry Vaughan – and to Hopkins in the nineteenth, whose work she found marvellous for the way in which 'it describes all the stages in the struggle from obscurity to clarity; it does not simply celebrate the great moments of pure vision'. The prevalence of compassion and the possibility of absolution offered within Hopkins's poetry provided a model for her own work, bolstering her faith in poetry's ability to restore: 'Each vision of God is like a recovery, a winning-back of some lost state' (*Every Changing Shape*). As Emma Mason has argued, 'What Jennings learns from Hopkins, as she does from Wordsworth and Weil, is the dexterity to tumble through misery, grief, dejection, fear and loneliness as a way of accessing joy and stillness.'

Discussing the style of religious poetry she perceived Geoffrey Hill to be developing by 1960, Jennings cites R.P. Blackmur's comment on Emily Dickinson: 'What is behind the words or beyond them, we cannot know as facts [...] it is a bare statement amounting to vision – vision being a kind of observation of the ideal.' This seems a useful counterpoint to Jennings's brand of religious poetry. Occasionally, in poems such as 'Song for a Departure' and 'A Requiem', she strikes a note similar to that of an Emily Dickinson poem, evincing a startling confidence of abstract understanding, coupled with deep feeling and emotional affect – yet Jennings's poems are always more fleshed out. In her poems on explicitly Christian subjects, even when her speakers are consciously striving to cross the boundary between the real and the ideal, the language and imagery remain embodied: worldly, social, domestic, human. 'It is a human child she loves / Though a god stirs beneath her breast / And great salvations grip her side', concludes 'The Annunciation'; both this poem and 'Teresa of Avila' offer portraits of saintly women embracing the physical world. This focus on embodied experience was perhaps a direct consequence of Jennings's Roman Catholicism, in which 'incarnation, taking flesh, implies a profound horror not only of abstractions but also of all that is impersonal [...]. Poetry, like Christianity, preserves, when it is in a healthy state, the sense of personality and the dignity of being human' (*Poetry To-day*, p. 55).

In the nineteenth-century poets, and particularly in Matthew Arnold, Jennings perceived how doubt, as much as faith, could power religious poetry. 'Dover Beach', she suggested in her introduction to *The Batsford Book of Religious Verse*, is 'a great poem, a tragic cry which has the poignancy of apparently unanswered prayer'. The voices of religious poets in her own century were, she acknowledged, 'voices of people "crying in the wilderness". Nonetheless they have, particularly in the case of Eliot, cast some radiance over areas of doubt, unbelief and fear'. In her own work, the poem can contain or give form to prayer, as in 'On a Friend's Relapse and Return to a Mental Clinic', which shifts from reflection to petition ('O heal my friend. / [...] Bring her an end // Of suffering, or let us all protest / And realise / It is the good who often know joy least'), or 'Let There Be' (a direct invocation to Christ), or 'A Litany for Contrition'. It can also be an act of praise and celebration, as in the brief, uncomplicated poems 'Friendship' and 'Almost', or the more subtle and 'obstinate' lyric 'Against the Dark', which asserts that, because the fundamental impulse to poetry 'rises from the root of light', poems 'must praise // Even when grief is threatening, even when hope / Seems as far as the furthest star'.

'It is, I think, in my own poetry / I meet my God. He's a familiar there.' In poems such as 'A Way to a Creed', Jennings offers her own voice and insights, yet she objected to the term 'confessional poet' that had been readily applied to her American contemporaries Robert Lowell (also a Roman Catholic), Sylvia Plath and Anne Sexton, writing in her introduction to the 1987 *Collected Poems*: 'Art is not self-expression while, for me, "confessional poetry" is almost a contradiction in terms.' She resisted the equation of poetry and psychological turmoil that the term 'confessional' often seemed to imply. Part of her resistance may stem from her early associations of Confession (with a capital 'c') with 'shamefulness', 'terrors' and the 'wordless fears' alluded to in 'About These Things':

> [...] Maybe I am dumb
> Because if fears were spoken I would lose
>
> The lovely languages I do not choose
> More than the darknesses from which they come.

'Unlike Plath,' Michael Schmidt has argued, 'Jennings does not allegorise the causes for her mental disturbance. Poetry is not exorcism but sacrament, a sharing.' Her poems tread a line between 'I' and 'we', the particular and the universal. In poems such as 'A Depression' and the oft-anthologised 'One Flesh', the element of surprise derives from the unexpected shift from an objective to a subjective mode – from the experience of the other ('she', 'he' and 'they'), relayed by an impersonal narrator, to the lyric 'I'.

Conversely, in the collections most vulnerable to autobiographical interpretations – *Recoveries* and *The Mind Has Mountains* – the poems maintain for the most part a generalised perspective, focusing (as in 'Sequence in Hospital') on other people and on the workings of abstract emotional states ('this huge, vague fear'). The writing is motivated by empathy, compassion and communion, not by an urge to revelation or absolution for the individual. If lyrics such as the candid 'After a Time' come close to 'confessing' unrefined, autobiographical truths, they do so in a spirit of existential enquiry that extends well beyond the confines of personal experience, and do not seek to resolve, or absolve – only to acknowledge and communicate the difficult reality of being unsure.

Jennings was fundamentally interested in poetry as a mechanism through which experiences could be 'considered, refined, transformed', yielding truth through artfulness ('Any Poet's Epitaph'). Her poems celebrate life's sustaining energies (love, faith, art, the seasons) and the worldly manifestations of transcendent powers (water, music, light, stars; God, nature and creation). The final poem in this selection, which was the final poem in Jennings's last published collection, is an apt reflection of a poet whose mental world was irreparably damaged by her early experience of organised religion, and who was ultimately sustained by her personal faith in a Christian God and in the spiritual power of creativity. Jennings claimed that her poetry was a development of her religion; for her, both were routes to discovery. Her assertion, in 1961, of what poetry is for remained true throughout her life: 'What the poem discovers – and this is its chief function – is order amid chaos, meaning in the middle of confusion, and affirmation at the heart of despair.'

In making this selection I have attempted to reflect the range of Jennings's preoccupations, as well as the forms, styles and tones that seem to me characteristic of the various phases of her poetic trajectory. In a few instances I have chosen poems because they are atypical, and so hint at alternative directions her work might have taken. I am grateful to Michael Schmidt, who knew Jennings personally and knows her poetry intimately, for his guidance and for inviting me to undertake this project. Acknowledgement is also due to the editors and critics whose work has granted me access to Jennings's poetry and its various contexts; my main sources are listed in the following bibliography.

Select Bibliography

Jennings, Elizabeth, *The Collected Poems*, ed. Emma Mason (Manchester: Carcanet, 2012).

——, *New Collected Poems*, ed. Michael Schmidt (Manchester: Carcanet, 2002).

——, *Selected Poems* (Manchester: Carcanet, 1979).

——, *Every Changing Shape: Mystical Experience and the Making of Poems* (Manchester: Carcanet, 1996; first published 1961).

——, *Let's Have Some Poetry!* (London: Museum Press, 1960).

——, *Poetry To-day (1957-60)* (London: Published for The British Council by Longmans, Green, 1961).

—— (ed.), *The Batsford Book of Religious Verse* (London: Batsford, 1981).

BBC Radio 4, *Desert Island Discs*, 8 January 1993 (audio recording; available online at substitute https://www.bbc.co.uk/sounds/play/p0093x99).

Gramang, Gerlinde, *Elizabeth Jennings: An Appraisal of Her Life as a Poet, Her Approach to Her Work and a Selection of the Major Themes of Her Poetry* (Lampeter: The Edwin Mellen Press, 1995).

Greene, Dana, *Elizabeth Jennings: 'The Inward War'* (Oxford: OUP, 2018).

Schmidt, Michael, *Lives of the Poets* (London: Phoenix, 1999).

Index of Titles and First Lines

First lines are shown in *italic*, titles in roman.